Chapter One

Understanding the Virus

MEAN ANGRY
DEMANDING Unrealistic
MICRO-MANAGER Stubborn
"SELF-CENTERED"
UNWILLING TO ACCEPT CHANGE **Spoiled**
Obnoxious BLUNT
SELF-ABSORBED RUDE

B RIDEZILLA

"B" is for...

The word "bridezilla" was created in the 1990's as a humorous description of a woman who unknowingly transforms herself into a frightening, threatening, prehistoric creature while planning her wedding. This once humorous word is now considered to be demeaning and hurtful. A woman referred by others as a bridezilla is synonymous with a woman who is difficult, obnoxious, controlling, or extreme. "Wedding-perfection-itis" or better known as the bridezilla virus is a disease which causes a transformation to begin within the bride who wants her wedding to be perfect. Unfortunately, the bridezilla virus is not limited to the bride herself. No one is immune from this disease. Mutated strains of the bridezilla virus appear in the form of "Momzilla," "Bridesmaidzilla," "MOHzilla" (Maid of honor) and even "Groomzilla."

Every bride is infected with some form or strain of the bridezilla virus. It is believed that the virus is released when the engagement ring is placed on the ring finger. The virus lays dormant until such time stress triggers the disease and the bridezilla virus emerges. The virus may strike at any time prior to, during, or even after the wedding. Severe symptoms of the virus most often emerge closer to the wedding day with the most extreme symptoms occurring on the wedding day itself.

There are several warning signs that may appear which signify that the virus is present. The symptoms may include a person being:

- Stubborn
- Unrealistic
- Unwilling to accept substitutions or change
- Demanding
- Difficult to rationalize
- Obnoxious
- Self- centered
- Angry
- Micro manager
- Alienate friends, family, significant other.
- Mean
- Rude

Once a bride has contracted the virus handle with extreme care. Being informed and able to cope with the various symptoms will allow the bride, bridal party, family, and friends to enjoy the couple's most special day.

Are weddings all about the bride?

Calling the wedding day "the bride's special day" is not entirely a true statement. Last time I checked you need a groom/significant other to complete the couple. Placing the emphasis on the bride increases pressure for the bride and/or the brides' family to produce a flawless event. Most of the time the groom/significant other is not mentioned and is merely referred to as a puzzle piece needed to complete the couple.

A wedding celebration traditionally focuses on the bride, but a wedding is for the groom, the parents, the grandparents, your siblings, friends, and various other individuals I failed to mention. So why do we then focus only on the bride? My best answer is that the wedding planning process is most often left to the bride or brides' family. It may also be due to the fact that the bride wants her fairy tale wedding that only she can plan what she wants. The groom/significant other usually have little to no interest in the planning process. As long as the bride is happy, then the statement- "it's all about the bride" will be used.

Get Vaccinated

The simplest way to prevent the bridezilla virus from occurring is to go on a "wedding date" with your fiancé. The main focus of the wedding date is to have time alone to talk about your wedding celebration. On your date, do something where you will have no outside influences affecting your decisions as a couple. Discuss and decide together on what you want your wedding celebration to be.

A few of the questions to ask and answer about your wedding are:

- What day would like to get married?
- Where would you like to be married?
- What type of wedding would you like to have?
- What time of day would you like the ceremony to be performed?
- How many guests would you like to attend?

- How much can we afford to spend on a wedding?
- How many attendants would you like stand up?
- What type of food would you like to serve?
- What colors or theme would you like to have?
- What type of entertainment?

Once you get a few questions answered and have an idea of your wedding style, the next step is to think back to the weddings you have attended and make a list of the items you disliked. This will help you plan your wedding with your guests in mind and keep the guest complaints to a minimum.

Top guest complaints:

- Inconvenient wedding date
- Not knowing where to go/ no map or directions
- Waiting for the ceremony to begin
- Not enough seating for ceremony
- Too much time between ceremony and reception
- Too large of distance from ceremony to reception
- No seating chart/ seated with strangers
- Long speeches
- Bad dining experience- cold or lack of food
- No knowledge of a Cash bar or poor bar service
- Music too loud / Inappropriate music type
- Room temperature- too hot or too cold
- Cramped spaces or too spacious
- Centerpieces obstructing views
- Ungracious hosts
- Disorganization and lulls
- Left without a ride for out of town guests
- Badly behaved bridal party

By discussing each of your wants, needs, and expectations you both will be better prepared to answer and defend your decisions you have made as a couple to your family and friends. At this part of the event planning, everyone will have an opinion and will try to give you advice. With your plans laid out and family informed, the wedding planning process will be easier to execute and less stressful.

The Three C's of Wedding Planning

The process of wedding planning can be a difficult, exhausting task. Often planning a wedding becomes a second job. Many believe the three "C's" of wedding planning is cut, color, or carat weight. Although these are important, the three C's of wedding planning is communication, cooperation, and consideration.

Communication, cooperation, and consideration are the building blocks or foundation for a successful wedding/event. The combination of the three C's is the only known vaccine available to soften the bridezilla virus symptoms.

If we learn to practice the three C's, wedding planning would be virtually stress free. Unfortunately, during the wedding planning process most brides forget or neglect to use the three C's. When this occurs, it is often done subconsciously to fill the need to create the "perfect" wedding instead of a family celebration.

Communication is important to express your wants, needs, and concerns. You need to cooperate with others to achieve a successful event. You must be considerate of others feelings, responsibilities, knowledge, and liabilities. Concentrate on these three C's and you will have the most amazing, memorable event with little or no stress.

Our marriage...Their wedding!

During the wedding planning process, family and friends love to voice their opinions, views, and wants. Rather than having hurt feelings, uncomfortable confrontation, or angry individuals: you give in to their ideas to keep the peace. Most often this temporary fix only adds fuel to smoldering embers igniting them into a roaring fire of disappointment and stress. It may be your marriage, but it has become their wedding. The bridezilla virus waits for this opportunity to occur so it can infect everyone it can. Remember, they are happy for you, want only the best for you, and in their mind the "best" is what they are suggesting and/or doing.

When family and friends intercede with suggestions, it is best to schedule another "wedding" date with your fiancé. Discuss the proposed changes, the monetary requirements, and possible solutions. When you have come to a decision on the suggested ideas, you are then able to confront the individuals in a calm, stress-free way to advise them of your plans. Remind them how much you appreciate their enthusiasm, and genuine concern they have for your event.

A little schmoozing goes a long way to keep the bridezilla virus from surfacing prematurely. It is difficult to please everyone. If you at least consider their suggestions, wants, and needs of others, you will be seen as cooperative (even if you do not use a single suggestion.) This way others feel that they are contributing to the celebration and you are able to keep your plans without hurt other's feelings.

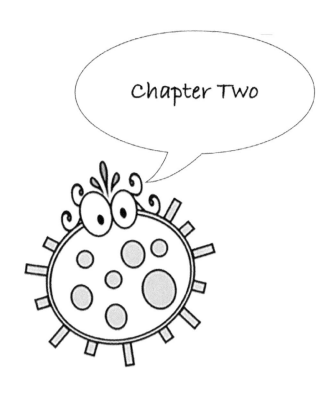

Champagne Wishes,
caviar dreams, then a dose of reality

Contests, Drawings, and Expo's ...oh my!

As I stood in front of the magazine rack of a local store, I realized that many of the bridal magazines, wedding planning guides, and DIY weddings books offer a variety information. Wedding shows or expos give the newly engaged or seasoned bride-to-be an opportunity to have personal contact with multiple vendors.

Wedding shows can be a wedding planning overload to your senses. Vendors participating in a wedding show or expo are specialists in their individual fields. With multiple vendors in one location it is easy to comparison shop, ask questions, and gather information on their services.

So how do you swim in a sea of vendors? The answer is to go slow, steady, and tread lightly. If you jump in you may drown with information overload which may cause the bridezilla virus will surface prematurely.

To achieve a successful wedding show outing:

- **Create a special email address** only for wedding information – this frees up your personal email from all of the advertising wedding emails vendors will send you from the company hosting the show.
- **Bring labels** with your name, address, phone, wedding date, and email address for prize drawings.
- **Wear comfortable shoes**. It is not a fashion show. Shopping for the best vendor(s) to fit your wedding plan is time consuming and you will be doing a lot of walking. The bridezilla virus will certainly surface if your feet hurt.
- **Wear comfortable clothing**. There are usually samples of wedding cake, food, snacks, and drinks at a show/expo for the tasting.
- **Bring friends, family, or bridal party** with you to share in the experience. If you are just starting your wedding planning it may be best to attend with your fiancé to avoid outside opinions.
- **Make a plan.** Make of list of what you are shopping for. It should ease any anxiety from wedding planning overload.

One last piece of advice…. Go the show/expo hungry. Forget the diet…. eat, drink, and have fun!

#getting married

You're engaged and you want to announce it the world. Social media is the easiest and fastest way to do it. Dozens of emails, messages, tweets, and snaps put your wedding out into the world for many to comment, judge, and offer support as well as unwanted criticism. Social media can help, but most often hurt the bride's feelings which can fuel the bridezilla virus to emerge. The best defence against an infection is to be in control of your social media with a wedding website.

Wedding websites have become a standard addition to the wedding planning process. A wedding website can be a practical tool to help inform others of your wedding plans. Most wedding websites are free to create and you decide on the amount of information to share.

Now that the word is out (that you are getting married) many of the same questions will be asked. People are excited for you and want to know how as much information as possible. At first it is wonderful to share the stories, but after a few dozen times, you begin to get annoyed, short tempered, and are perceived to be a "B." Your actions may be misread as the onset of the bridezilla virus but it is only frustration.

A wedding website is a wonderful way to tell your story, post pictures you want seen, and advise your wedding guests on wedding updates without sounding pushy or obsessive. Be careful not to give too much information away but some items you may want to include are:

- Story of the proposal
- Story of your relationship
- Date of the wedding
- Countdown clock (optional)
- Directions to wedding ceremony/reception for wedding guests
- Wedding party bio's
- Hotel information
- Transportation options for out of town guests
- Wedding timelines and updates
- Menu options- may also be a help for those with food allergies
- Gift Registry information
- Suggestion Board

A suggestion board is a wonderful way to allow friends and family to give you suggestions and ideas without putting you in an uncomfortable position of hurting anyone's feelings. You can graciously accept or decline the suggestions and ideas without fear of a label of a "b...." word.

Social media has put additional stress on a bride to provide wedding board pins, create clever hashtags, and post multiple photos. At times, friends and family will try to be helpful and post items that you have not approved. Social media can help and at the same time hurt an event.

To avoid the most popular mistakes of social media, a bride should avoid the following:

- **Posting Incessantly**. Save something for the wedding. Do not give everything away before the big day.
- **Using social media on your wedding day**. You must be present on your wedding day. NO SELFIES... NO POSTING!
- **Losing it with hashtags**. Unless the hashtag makes sense, do not get out of control. No one cares.
- **Going off on Facebook**. Never talk badly about any one (family, friends, or vendors) on Facebook. It makes you appear to be affected by the bridezilla virus and a bit psycho.
- **Getting too sappy**. Everyone knows you love your fiancée; there is no need to boost it on social media.
- **Going radio silent**. Do not be an elusive bride. Give people what they want, the essentials. Any more is too much.
- **Letting people use social media during the ceremony**. This is a special time for the wedding couple, letting others post or allowing them to be pocket photographers is distracting. You paid for a photographer to capture the moment, do not let others get in their way.
- **Continuous selfies**. Seriously, no one wants to see a selfie of you every day until the wedding.

I don't think so!

When you become engaged, having a disagreement or an argument is inevitable. Most arguments will stem from stress and frustration stemming from the disease. The bridezilla virus has an ugly side that likes to ignite fires of doubt, self-worthlessness, and fear within the bride. Don't let the virus get you down. Inoculate with knowledge, conquer with organization and eliminate with communication.

Your fiancé may not be helping with the wedding planning and this may reflect in your mind as not caring. On the contrary, your fiancé may be saying "whatever you want dear" as a way of making you happy. Your significant other does not want to see you stressed or upset nor do they want to make you stressed or upset. This may be their way of helping. In their minds it is easier to give in to your suggestions than disagree. They are just trying to give you everything you wanted. Remember, most men never even thought of their wedding day. This is very new for them and they are doing the best they can to understand the wedding planning process.

Another area where disagreements may occur is with your parents. Parents wants what is best for their child but they also want the wedding to be a reflection them. This is especially true if they are paying for the event. Parents often negate your plans if they are not up to their expectations. It is difficult for a bride to step in and tell them "no" to any additions or suggestions especially if they are paying the bill. The pressure and guilt from parents to host a "perfect" wedding may lead you to feel you are an inadequate wedding planner and need their help. At this point, the bridezilla virus will begin to grow and it can only be stopped by actively communicating your concerns, wants, and needs.

Brides become self-absorbed with wedding planning. Everyone wants their wedding is unique, special, and memorable. Weddings have become a competition between friends, co-workers, and even family members. Many brides feel that from their engagement to the wedding day, she should be the center of attention. It is about "her" wedding and nothing else. When the brides are rolling their eyes, huffing, ignoring the conversation, or swaying the conversation towards their wedding, the onset of the bridezilla virus is possible.

The bridezilla virus has been proven to be the cause of broken friendships and hurt feelings between the bride and her bridesmaids. Allowing the bridezilla virus to emerge and infect those closest to you during planning process will leave you alone, angry, and bitter. Be open to criticism, humbled by complements, and thankful you have friends in your life that stand by your side to witness and celebrate your marriage.

When the bridezilla virus strikes, the bride's friends and family are not the only victims, vendors are often targets too. The attacks against vendors are usually harmless but some have been known to be serious.

Vendors are just trying to provide the services requested by the couple. The talented individuals hired to bring the couples vision of their wedding day into reality should be treated with respect A wedding is more than a sale to most vendors. It is a labor of love to create a special day for the couple. It is as important to them, as it is for the couple, to get it "right."

Brides who have gone past the point of no return begin to act poorly. Badly behaved brides have been known to contact vendors at all hours of the day or night, demand attention even if the vendor is unavailable, request services that are not listed in the wedding contract for free, or even threaten nonpayment of services if they do not get what they want. Often badly behaved brides blame the vendors for miscommunication when the something doesn't go her way. Often the bride did not clearly express her vision to the vendor, a change was submitted by someone else (Mom) who contacted the vendor on the bride's behalf, or the couple changed their mind without notifying the vendor. With the electronic era, personal interaction has almost been eliminated.

A badly behaved bride now feels empowered through social media to broadcast to the world her side of a situation that did not go her way. Never will a badly behaved bride post, tweet, or tell the entire truth of a situation that does not put her in the best possible position. It may take an

Intervention from their significant other to intercede with the wedding planning until the bride has recovered from the bridezilla virus.

Not quite what I would pick

You invited your friends, family, and loved ones to share in your special day. Deciding as a couple how you would like to celebrate your day is an amazing and joyous time. Unfortunately, invited guests, friends, and family will have certain expectations when attending your wedding. Some of their expectations may or may not be a part of your wedding plan. Everyone is different and it is impossible to please everyone. When a person voices an opinion or simply states *"that is not what I would do"* it can be hurtful and demeaning. It is impossible not to have hurt feelings or become defensive when someone is talking poorly about your wedding plan/celebration. This is a special day for you and your fiancé, your wedding is a very personal reflection of the two of you.

How does one become a wedding critic? People judge others often because they are comparing themselves to another person. Some experts believe it is a survival technique. Comparing ourselves with others makes the person comparing feel good about themselves.

Can you stop judging others? It is very unrealistic to believe that this can be done. When you are about to judge others, take a moment to think about the judgment you are about to pass. Remember, the event you are attending is <u>not</u>

your event. If the host(s) is happy, then the event is a success. Their decisions may not be one you would have made, but if it is right for the couple, it's the right choice. Accept what is and not what you would have done.

Many would say that any criticism isn't worth dwelling on. Try your best to block out the negativity of others, compromise with people that are important to you, and do not agree to anything that makes you feel uncomfortable to keep peace among family and friends.

Budget or busted?

Creating a budget is an easy task to complete. Sticking to a budget is the most difficult task to master. A wedding celebration can make or break a couple financially. Dating back to the First Epistle of Timothy in the New Testament

(1 Timothy 6:10, KJV): "For the love of money is the root of all kinds of evil." Often this quote is misquoted by saying "money is the root of all evil." Money would then be perceived as the source or root of all evil in the world which is not true. It's not the money's fault, don't blame it! It's good to have money. I like money, on some days it multiples in my wallet and other times it runs off with other money never to be seen again.

Starting a marriage in debt from hosting a wedding is never a good idea. When debt becomes overwhelming the bridezilla virus develops on a much quicker level.

So how do you prevent the bridezilla virus from developing over money issues? One way is to decide on how much money you have available to spend on the wedding celebration.

The following is an example of a budget breakdown range of

wedding expenses:

- Venue – from 5% - 13%
  - Including facility fees for both ceremony and reception locations
  - Marriage Officiate fee, wedding license fee, transportation fee
- Food / Beverage – from 30% - 64%
  - Including appetizers, dinner, cake, candy table, sweet table, beverages (alcohol and non-alcoholic selections)
- Photography / Video – from 10% - 16%
  - Including photographer's fees, proofs, flash drives, wedding albums
  - Table size
- Entertainment – from 5% - 15%
  - Including ceremony, dinner, and reception entertainment (band, DJ, photo booth, etc.)
- Rentals – from 3% - 17%
  - Including chairs, tables, linens
- Flowers / Decorations – from 6% - 12%
  - Including ceremony, reception, and personal flowers
  - Candles, vases, wedding favors, invitation, postage

What is not incorporated in the budget breakdown is all of the other items needed for a successful wedding celebration: the wedding dress, wedding dress accessories, wedding dress alterations, beauty essentials, tuxedo rentals (must include the groom/significant other), rings, attendant's gifts, and gratuities. Nothing is more frustration that planning an event and not having enough money to cover the expenses. Since all of the above items are necessary for a successful wedding and a happy bride, I suggest adding additional categories to the wedding budget:

- Bridal beauty
- Gifts/gratuities.

The bridal beauty category includes all of the items for the bride herself including preparation for the wedding day (hair, nails, make-up, massage, facials, tanning, dental), wedding dress, wedding rings, jewelry, dress alterations and accessories. It is very easy to get carried away with the bridal beauty category. If you feel beautiful you will emit a "bridal glow." The inner glow of happiness shines through only when the bridezilla virus is dormant.

A desired wedding look takes time, planning, and preparation. Some women wake up with a natural beauty and need no enhancement. Secretly we do not like you (just kidding) but we really want to be you. Your wedding day is no exception. With a little time, practice, and preparation all brides can be relaxed, beautiful, and feel their best on the "big" day. Brides beware…. IF you do not take steps to prepare for your bridal beauty you will unleash the bridezilla virus with a vengeance.

So just how do you figure a bridal beauty budget? Research, a good excel sheet, a timeline, and an open mind will guide you to determining your budget. As with any budget, start by listing the items you want and attach a price to each item. Add up the total of each price listed and you have the amount you would need for a budget to have the items you want. If the total amount shown is not workable, you can downgrade or eliminate items to fit your ideal targeted budget.

Staying organized

Starting the wedding planning process is an exciting time. A wedding is one of the most important life events to plan and execute. It takes commitment, dedication, and organization to keep the bridezilla virus from surfacing. To keep your head on straight as you plan your epic event there are several tips to keep the bridezilla virus dormant.

1. **Write everything down.** Make a list of everything that needs to be taken care of in no particular order. To get yourself organized, go through the list and prioritize the items that need to be taken care of first, second, etc.
2. **Consider a color coding system**. Buy a calendar or monthly planner exclusively for the wedding. Next, assign a color code for each vendor. When meeting with vendors, use the planner to schedule appointments, deposit due dates, follow-up emails, etc. in the chosen vendor color. By color coding your vendors, you will be able to see at a glance what is needed for who and when.

Note: Don't be afraid to ask you vendors to schedule the necessary appointments in advance to keep your wedding planning on track. As the wedding day approaches, your calendar will fill up quickly. By pre-scheduling your appointments you will not forget one!

3. **Communicate clearly**. Email subject lines need to be friendly, professional, and focused. The recipient should know by the subject line what to expect and understand that the email is somewhat urgent. You can use the body of the email to get personal.

4. **Start early**. It takes time to research your wedding plan. Procrastination only leads to the bridezilla virus surfacing prematurely.

5. **Plan to plan**. Make a plan to develop a plan. Thinking that everything will just magically come together "eventually" is totally false. A plan of action gets things done.

6. **Store all of your wedding items in one place.** Purchasing items for your wedding will be a continuous process. Where do you put everything until it is needed? The secret to organization is to pack these items according to the area that they are needed.

7. **Color code once again**. Assign the areas in which the purchased items are needed (ceremony, reception, cake, personal, etc.) Next, assign a color for each location that items are needed. Place a color sticker on the boxes with the location and time needed for delivery in the assigned color. This way when it comes time to take the items to the designated locations, you are able to do this efficiently by looking at color then item. The last few days prior to the wedding day are filled with numerous tasks. Trying to find misplaced items you purchased for the wedding is frustrating, time consuming and a breeding zone for the bridezilla virus to grow.

Beginning a basic plan to stay organized with your wedding planning will help avoid the virus from appearing prematurely. By designating specific time to the planning process you will free up time closer to the wedding day to relax, decompress, and stay focused on the true meaning of the celebration... your commitment to each other.

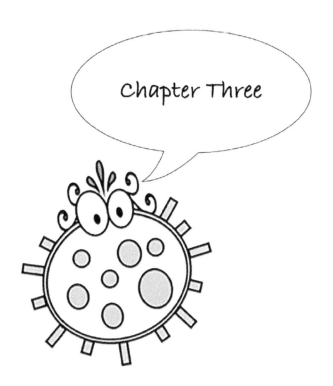

Be Our Guest...

Do I know you???

After the initial excitement of the proposal and the actual wedding planning had begun, the next step is to determine who to invite to the celebration. A wedding is a family event. Creating a guest list is a jigsaw puzzle with multiple people each having a puzzle piece that is needed to complete the game.

The best way to create a guest list with little or no issues is to follow the basic rule of thirds. The rule of thirds divides the guest list between your family, your fiancé's family, and the wedding couple. Problems arise when one of the guest lists has gone over the allotted guest amount. Even more problems arise when the person with the extended guest list states that they will pay for the additional people so that they may attend the event. This is not only unfair but it is a way of having your family high jack your wedding. In addition, the bridezilla virus has been known to affect various family members as well as the bride while gathering the guest list.

Keeping a guest list in perspective to the wedding budget is harder than balancing the national debt. Friends, family, co-workers, and people you barely know will expect to be invited to the wedding celebration. Your wedding budget will be blown if you do not set some ground rules.

The easiest and most effective way of preparing a guest list is to have a combined family gathering. This should be a relaxed, fun-filled event with little to no wedding pressure. Sometime throughout the gathering, sit down and express some guest concerns. Address your preferences when it comes to inviting children, co-workers, ceremony only guests, casual acquaintances, and plus ones. Once everyone is on the same page then you can introduce the concept of the "police lineup." When you are agonizing over to invite or not invite a person on your list, ask yourself if you could recognize them in a police lineup. If the answer is no, then do not invite them. It's that simple.

If you are unable to balance the "guest budget" it is time to pull out the calculator and show everyone in black and white the costs involved to invite a guest to the wedding. To achieve this amount, simply take your total wedding budget amount and divide by the number guests you are planning to invite.

Example- $10,000 budget / 200 people = $50 per person

While creating a guest list, some friends, family, and co-workers will have hurt feelings for not being invited to the wedding. Unfortunately, this is unavoidable but it can be less of an issue if you take some precautions. Explain to the uninvited guests that you wanted to have everyone be a part of your wedding celebration but it is financially impossible. Explain that you would like to have a private, less formal celebration with your "special" guests. This may soften the blow of not being invited to the actual wedding celebration.

Brides beware; the bridezilla virus may infect family members during the guest list creation. Mothers of the wedding couple will have strong opinions on who should be and who will be invited. To keep the bridezilla virus from infecting the moms plan to meet with them separately to thank them for their contribution to the wedding planning and guest list suggestions. Stress that you appreciate their enthusiasm and excitement for the celebration. State that you understand that they want to share this special event with you. Gently tell them that you would love to have everyone be invited to the wedding but it is not possible unless the wedding budget was increased by the calculated amount. Hopefully the virus will bypass your moms if you initiate preventative moves.

Paper trail

A wedding invitation is more than an announcement of your upcoming nuptials; it sets the tone and level of formality of the event. A wedding invitation may be whimsical, traditional, contemporary, or even electronic. In any event, the wedding invitation introduces the guest to the all-important first impression of your wedding.

Wedding invitations have evolved from a wedding being typically announced by means of a <u>Town crier</u> (a man who would walk through the streets announcing in a loud voice the news of the day) to beautifully crafted paper with elegant script announcing the event. With the electronic era, wedding announcements have taken a new twist and can been sent via email.

Choosing your invitation type may be overwhelming which can

cause the bridezilla virus to surface during the invitation selection process. It may also appear during the ordering process, addressing, and mailing processes.

Once you have found that special invitation, deciding on the enclosures is another issue. You can go crazy and turn your invitation into a book filled with added pages of information if you are not careful.

The typical invitation includes:

- The invitation with two envelopes (outer and inner)
- The reception card
- The response card
- The response card envelope (which requires postage)
- Additional pages and cards that provide directions, hotel information, even gift registry information.

Shopping for wedding invitations can be a costly mistake if you are not careful. To help avoid costly mistakes and to keep the bridezilla virus tame consider the following points:

- The number of invitations does not equal the number of guests. Married couples and families receive one invitation
- Knowing the invitation count gives you the total number of thank you cards, RSVP cards, and wedding stationery needed.
- Cost per invitation will vary on the quantity and quality of materials used.
- Enclosures that are added will increase the cost of postage by added weight to the envelope
- Addressing services will add to the cost but will save you hours of tedious inscription.
- Postage is not limited to the outer envelope; response cards must have postage.
- Hidden costs will always be present. Here are a few "hidden" costs that may occur:
  - Special Ink (for the DIY invites)

- Proofs – a proof is necessary to avoid misspelled words, incorrect addresses, and wrong times.
- Custom colors, special fonts, special paper will increase the cost
- Odd-shaped envelopes & unique fasteners add bulk and weight to the invitation; it may also add a special handling fee by the post office.

Purchasing and creating your wedding invitations will be just the start of your paper trail. When ordering, I suggest you order you thank you notes along with your invitations. Purchasing all of the needed wedding stationery at one time will save you additional shipping costs and it will in turn allow you to pre-address thank you notes to save you time after the wedding. Not ordering enough items will add an additional set-up cost, and add several weeks to receive your invitations. If you are ready to send out your invitations but still need a few more to go out, I highly suggest you wait to send out the entire guest list at one time. No one wants to receive and invitation days or even weeks after everyone else.

It is always a good idea to purchase a few extra invitations to allow for errors. I suggest purchasing extra envelopes as well. Most times an error occurs while addressing the envelope. Having extra envelopes will keep your error unnoticed. Unused envelopes may be used after the wedding.

Chapter Four

Saying "Yes"
(The Essentials)

Dress + Diet = Disaster

Since the engagement, most brides have been impatiently waiting to go dress shopping. Shopping for your wedding dress makes you feel like a bride. Before you run out to the bridal shop, take a moment and consider the following.

First and most importantly, take a good look in the mirror. This is the person your fiancé fell in love with. Changing your appearance for the wedding will only bring out the inner bridezilla. Lack of food causes anyone to be cranky, throw in the stress of wedding planning and you will have a bride with full blown symptoms of the virus.

Entering into a life change should be done for personal health reasons and not to fit into a wedding dress. Most brides who transform their body for the wedding day return to their pre-diet size shortly after the nuptials. Crash diets or extreme measures to slim down may result in long term health issues, dull lifeless hair, and loose skin. You are beautiful just the way you are.

Shopping for a wedding dress can be both a wonderful and frightful experience. Choosing who will accompany the bride (better known as the "support team") to the shopping experience is just as important as the dress itself. Your support team members should be family or friends that are impartial. They should be individuals with whom you respect and value their opinion. They should not be opinionated, stubborn, or hot headed. Your support team should be just that -supportive.

Once your support team has been chosen, plan a dress shopping meeting, party, or girl's night. At this event your team members are able to meet and discuss wedding dress ideas that include dress style, type, color, and designers of wedding dresses that would complement the bride. A bride has a vision of herself in her dress on her wedding day. Often our bodies will not support our bridal vision. Keep in mind wedding dress ad models wear a size 2-4 whereas the average woman wears a size 12-14. It is a difficult and disappointing time when the bride realizes that their dream wedding dress does not fit her body or budget. Disappointment, criticism, and low self-esteem can be avoided if several steps are taken in advance.

Encourage your support team to share their opinions and preferences in this private setting and not on the showroom floor. This not only saves time but eliminates embarrassing comments and hurt feelings. The chance of the bridezilla virus surfacing has been lowered by preparing a dress buying game plan. Together as a team you can develop a design style that complements the bride.

Going clothes shopping, especially for a special occasion, may be frustrating, over whelming, and stressful. Many pieces of clothing look beautiful on a hanger but once tried on – horrible. Simply seeing ourselves stripped down to undergarments in a full length mirror, overhead florescent lighting can frighten us into never eating sweets again.

To keep wedding dress shopping a positive experience try the following:

• Make your dress appointment early in the day when sale

associates are fresh and cheerful.

- Try not to eat or drink before your appointment. Being bloated does not help with self-esteem.
- Wear undergarments that make you feel pretty, sexy, and special. No need for special shoes at this time.
- Bring a camera and have a member of your support team take pictures of you in each dress you try on. This is a wonderful way to see how you look in each dress and in photos. What we envision and what the camera sees are totally different. In addition, it is a great way to remember the day.
- When considering gown styles keep in mind the style of your venue. A ball gown may be out of place on a beach.
- Trust your instincts – you will know when to say "yes" to a dress.

A word of advice on dress shopping, do not have try-on trauma when you see the size label in your wedding dress. Wedding dress sizing has not been updated in decades. Over the year's women's body types have changed. Years ago clothes were tailored and rarely purchased off the rack which is no longer the norm. The size label in the dress does not matter; it is all about the fit.

Let's get physical!

I do believe once you have found your wedding dress you can enhance the areas that are exposed such as your arms, shoulders, back, neck, etc. This is in no way a substitution to adapting a healthy lifestyle or losing weight in a healthy way for personal reasons. Enhancing is an alternative to assist you to look and feel your best on your wedding day. Enhancing your body helps you to avoid disappointment which fuels the bridezilla virus. Most often the bride's arms are the first noticeable area to be firmed up. The most beautiful dress will look awful if your arms flap more than your lips. The next area would be the shoulders and chest areas. A corset or push up bra should push up your breasts and not fat. Since most wedding dresses are full length gowns there is no need firm or tone your legs except to build endurance for the long grueling wedding day.

Before starting a toning program, it is always best to check with your health care professional to avoid any future health issues. In addition, I do suggest you consult a professional fitness specialist to instruct you how to properly tone the targeted areas. Many times we consult the internet for toning exercises. Often this can be a waste of time and effort if the exercises are not the correct ones to achieve the desired

effect. Working out and seeing no visible results gets the bride frustrated, emotionally crippled, and discouraged which fuels the bridezilla virus to grow and develop.

Wrestling your underwire

The foundation is the most important part of a building. Likewise, a proper foundation is the most important part of the wedding attire. Nothing gets a woman crankier than the wrong choice of undergarments. Items that are too tight limit your air flow, discourage bending, and are uncomfortable. Items that are too loose give no support which allows body parts to travel at will. Not wearing foundation attire at all.... ewe! I understand being unrestricted and free on your wedding day but your dress should fit properly for a stress free day.

Once you purchase your wedding dress the next stop should be to a fine lingerie store to be professionally fit for the proper undergarments needed to make your wedding gown fit like a glove. Bring a picture of your gown to make sure you have the proper bra or corset. An ill-fitting underwire bra or corset can be the most painful, uncomfortable piece of clothing

ever worn. The underwire of a bra or corset was meant for uplifting support but somewhere throughout the years it has become an item of torture. Brides can go from zero to dangerously infected with the virus if her underwire does not lay properly.

Special consideration should also be for your choice of bathroom accessibility garments for the big day. Wear what you feel most comfortable which is an appropriate for style of dress along with the ability to use the restroom with ease.

Once your foundation is chosen, it is best to wear the items for an entire day. This test will let you know if you need to replace any uncomfortable items. Comfort is your goal for the wedding day as well as support. Be sure to bring the necessary foundation items to your dress alteration appointments. With a proper foundation, alterations should make your wedding dress fit like a glove.

Note: Foundation items need to be checked during the wedding dress alteration process. Any weight gain or loss will affect your foundation. Items may need to be replaced. The bridezilla virus will surface if you use foundation items that do not fit properly or is uncomfortable.

The Glass Slipper Syndrome

Once upon a time Prince Charming was dancing with Cinderella who was wearing a beautiful ball-gown complete with glass slippers. We never knew she was wearing these exquisite high heeled shoes until she revealed them. Imagine what her feet felt like the next day... sore!

Once your dress is chosen, foundation set, the next step is finding the perfect shoes. Most women consider comfort over style or price when shoe shopping, but when we are shopping for our wedding shoes brides do not mind a little discomfort for style. Achy feet enable the bridezilla virus to surface and grow. So why do brides constantly choose shoes style over comfort? I believe it is because shoes are just so darn pretty and can make us look taller, sexier, and we feel complete when added to our wedding ensemble.

When shopping for shoes to coordinate with your wedding dress, there are several considerations you should observe for a pain free day. No one wants sore feet before, during, or after their wedding. Brides should ask themselves several of the following questions before purchasing their wedding shoes:

- Will these shoes be seen?
    - If your shoes are not being seen go for comfort and a second pair for style.
- Are they comfortable when I first put them on?
    - You should never have to "break in" shoes it doesn't work.
- Is the fabric stretchable to allow for your feet to swell?
    - Your feet will swell during the day and your shoe needs to accommodate for this.
- Are your toes able to move or are they cramped together?
    - If you can't wiggle your toes in your shoes, the shoes are too tight!
- Are you able to walk easily on all surfaces without assistance?
    - The higher the heel the shorter the stride of your walk which in turn will increase foot pain.
- Is there any type of support in the shoe to allow you to wear this shoe for an extended period of time?
    - Add inserts to help cushion the heels, arches and balls of your feet for added comfort.
- Does this shoe stay on while walking or dancing?
    - A shoe with a strap will decrease the chance of foot injury and your dancing shoes will stay on for the day/night.

Still stuck on style? Just can't grasp the idea that comfortable shoes are wedding dress worthy? You can have the best of both worlds! By choosing a variety shoes aimed for specific times of your wedding will save your feet hours if not days of discomfort.

Start by creating a chart of "shoe" time. Begin with the start of your day and block off time that you would be wear a particular pair of shoes!

- Possibly start with flats/slippers before the ceremony
- Stylish heels for the actual ceremony
- Walking shoes for photos
- Reception and dancing shoes
- Finish with your original flats/slippers

Between shoe changes, it may be difficult to find someone to massage your feet. If a foot massage is not available, a tennis ball will be your best friend! When your feet are achy simply place a tennis ball on the ground, sit down, remove your shoe, and roll your foot from heel to toe and back over the tennis ball several times. By applying slight pressure while rolling your foot on the tennis ball you will give yourself an instant foot massage. A wedding is a marathon not a sprint. Throughout the course of the day several pairs of shoes are necessary to help keep the bridezilla virus dormant. Remember, by changing your shoes it will keep a spring in your step and hopefully a smile on your face.

It's Sew Perfect... or is it?

It's your wedding day; everything is just how you imagined and then a wardrobe malfunction. A broken bustle, stubborn zipper, stains, tears, loose strings and everything in between may release the bridezilla virus to infect you and everyone around. With proper preparation, these little mishaps can be handled with ease and your day can go on.

An emergency sewing kit should have the following:

- Large safety pins for a broken bustle
- Zipper ease or white crayon for a stuck zipper
- Tide to Go Pen or Shout Wipes for miscellaneous stains
- White chalk to cover miscellaneous stains
- Double sided tape to fix fallen hem

- Clean white terry-cloth towel to brush dirt away from bottom of dress
- Travel size garment steamer
- Q-tips
- Needle and thread
- Scissors
- Clear nail polish

If a spot occurs throughout the day, do not release the bridezilla virus! Stay calm and the Tide-to-Go pen will help, the white chalk will help cover most stains until you are able to get the dress professionally cleaned.

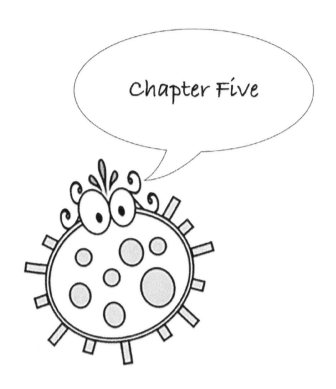

Always a bridesmaid...

Gossip Girls

Bridesmaids are very special addition to a wedding. In ancient times, according to folklore, bridesmaids were dressed alike to fool the evil spirits so the spirits could not dampen the marriage with bad luck. Today, bridesmaids dress in similar dresses, color, or style. They may not even match at all. One thing for sure, being a bridesmaid is both a blessing and a curse. Choosing who will be a bridesmaid is a difficult task that one should choose wisely and not in haste.

Bridesmaids should consist of close friends or family that can put up with you in any situation. They should know how to handle and guide you from stress. Bridesmaids can help the bridezilla virus emerge or lay dormant. Bridesmaids may also entice the virus to appear especially if there is conflict between bridesmaids. The old saying "one bad apple can spoil the whole bunch" is true for a wedding party. One disgruntle bridesmaid can unknowingly lead to a full blown case of the bridezilla virus among the entire wedding party.

Most likely these are individuals you chose to be your bridesmaids are ones that you spend time with separately and rarely do they ever meet as a group. Different personalities make life interesting but in a wedding party it created chaos. Everyone in your group agreed to be a part of your wedding and wants only the best for you and your fiancé.

One thing for sure is that everyone has an opinion and will voice it to your face or behind your back.

Once your bridesmaids are chosen, it is best to have a meet and greet girl's night. Similar to your wedding date with your fiancé, this gathering is a chance for your bridesmaids to meet in a neutral location. This is a wonderful opportunity to also discuss your wedding ideas, dress color, style, and monetary expectations. Being a bridesmaid is a costly endeavor. Let's face it: the bridesmaid dress is usually not one you can wear again. If you do wear it after the wedding let's hope no one else has it on! In addition to the dress/accessories, the costs continue with the bridal shower, travel costs (if any), bachelorette party, and wedding gift. Problems arise between bridesmaids when money is an issue; they dislike each other, or when the dress is ugly.

Most women are naturally competitive and most love to talk. If you do or say something that a woman does not like she will talk about it. If you have a group of women who dislike something, then entire wedding experience can be a nightmare. The bridezilla virus will lurk among unhappy bridesmaids and grow to epidemic proportion if not handled immediately.

Bridesmaids can be jealous of each other if the bride shows any favoritism, is skinny, beautiful, controlling or clueless. Just stay positive and remind them we are all different but share a common interest…. the wedding.

The Leader of the Pack

Being chosen as the leader of the pack (maid of honor) is a special honor, as implies the name. The maid of honor is that one person who is unconditionally supportive, trustworthy, and knows the bride inside and out. The maid of honor is the person who fills multiple roles during the wedding planning process and the wedding itself. The most important role the maid of honor plays is that of the monitor. The maid of honor is the one who can voice an opinion without fear. She is the one who can tell the bride she is getting out of hand.

The maid of honor becomes a therapist, go-for and go-to person, time keeper, fashion expert, party planner (bridal shower, bachelorette,) rule enforcer, and liaison between the bride and bridesmaids. In essence, the maid of honor is the lion tamer. This honored position in the wedding party is not for the light-hearted. It comes with pressure and stress to stand beside the bride during all aspects of wedding planning. The added stress and pressure of being the maid of honor may force the bridezilla virus to surface within her.

When this happens the maid of honor now becomes known as the "MOH-zilla."

MOH-zilla's are easier to diagnosis since they are usually not in direct contact with the bride when the virus appears. The MOH-zilla generally sees her position as maid of honor as a sign of power over the other bridesmaids. She is usually very demanding, does not listen to other bridesmaid suggestions, plans events to her liking without consulting the other bridesmaids, and will be a general schmooze to the bride with a smile on her face.

The only way for a MOH-zilla to be relieved of the virus is to have an intervention. The entire wedding party must meet and confront the MOH-zilla in a friendly, non-threatening location. At this time everyone must be able to express their concerns without fear of judgment or retribution. A solution to any underlying issues must be reached and implemented. Being a part of a wedding party is being a part of a team. A team works together, sticks together, and supports each other in good times and in bad. Once the maid of honor has been cured, the wedding planning may continue without any further incidents and a good time will be had by all.

Mini Me

Some couples want to incorporate children in their ceremony. Flower girls, ring bearers, page boys, miniature brides/grooms have adorned wedding parties for centuries. A flower girl symbolically leads the bride forward, from childhood to adulthood and from innocence to her roles of a wife and mother. The flower girl usually precedes the bride and may scatter rose petals down the aisle for the bride to walk on.

Children standing up in a wedding are adorable and help build the excitement of the bride's entrance. No one can resist watching a small child toddle down the aisle or race down as fast as they can burn off some energy along the way. A child in the wedding party can be an asset or a liability.

Having a child in wedding could be a stressful situation which would allow the bridezilla virus to flare up unexpectedly. Children are unpredictable and not always controllable. Even the most well behaved child may have a moment of insanity. What is most forgotten about having a child in a wedding party is that most children are on a schedule. They eat at a certain time, eat certain foods, takes scheduled naps, have play time, and go to bed at a designated hour. Any deviation from their schedule and it becomes possible for unfavorable behavior to occur in addition to the bridezilla virus.

To place a child in a stressful, chaotic situation with strangers, unfamiliar surroundings, uncomfortable clothing,

and several hundred eyes watching their every move; a child is bound to act differently.

When a child acts up, runs around, or is disruptive during a wedding ceremony the bridezilla virus will spread like wild fire to all near the outburst. Most disruptive behavior occurs when a child is not watched or allowed to do things that normally would be denied.

Children require special attention from their parents, bride, and other wedding guests. Having a child be part of the wedding party is definitely their parent's responsibility and not yours. If you choose to involve a child be prepared for something to go wrong and accept the outcome without blame.

"Ruff" Time

Often before your significant other came into your life, a special furry friend was there meeting you at the door. Not only did they have to approve of your impending marriage, but your furry friend most likely barked/meowed in. Your fur baby is a part of your life and many couples want to include him/her in their wedding celebration. A wedding is a stressful time for the wedding couple and even more stressful for a pet.

Pets, namely dogs, are becoming increasingly popular to attend the wedding of their owners. Pets can be involved in many different ways from being included on the guest list to taking on a role in the bridal party.

Including your pet in your wedding celebration is a risk. To avoid a complete disaster from occurring (along with the bridezilla virus) plenty of planning and training must be done prior to the big event.

First, and most importantly, you must see if your venue will allow pets (other than service animals) on the property. An additional deposit, along with a waiver releasing the venue from any incidents including your pet may be

required if the pet is allowed. No one wants to be bitten by your pet on your wedding day.

Next you must ask yourself "Is my pet friendly towards people?" One or two guests at a time is an easier situation for the pet to adjust to. When hundreds of guests are present, your pet may be frightened, overwhelmed, or excited. They may not be the perfect little angel you see every day. Any time an animal feels uneasy it may result in disobedient, naughty or uncontrollable behavior which may be difficult to contain.

If you do decide to include your pet in your wedding celebration be sure to have the time to spend with your pet preparing them for the big day. This includes multiple trial runs at the venue, crowd conditioning, and additional obedience classes. You pet should be able to take direction from others since you and your significant other will be a bit busy on your wedding day.

If your pet is attending your big day, it is time to decide on their outfit or accessories. Most pets do not feel comfortable wearing clothing and they show this by trying to bite it off, or rub it off. Accessories should be kept to a minimum and properly sized. Ill-fitting articles may cause your pet harm. Choking hazards occur when your pet accessories are not well made. It is best to choose safety over style when dressing your pet.

Preserving the special moments with your pet is a challenge for your photographer. Pets add an additional level of stress for the photographer. It may be difficult to capture the moment when a pet is involved. Keep in mind that a pet will do things at will. In order for your photographer to be prepared for a pet photo, inform him/her as soon as possible. You may even want to consider taking an engagement photo with your pet to see how the pet handles the situation.

In addition, it will give the photographer an opportunity to get to know your pet and its personality.

It is also best to inform your guests that your pets will be attending the celebration. Any guests with allergies will have ample notice to bring any medication necessary to eliminate any symptoms that would ruin their day.

Regardless of how the pet is being included in the wedding celebration, you will need to provide a pet sitter for the time your pet is at the festivities. This person will be responsible for picking up your pet from your home or kennel, provide water, food, and treats, clean up any accidents, and return them back home or to the kennel.

A wedding is a stressful environment and your pet may not like or want the attention. Being photographed, chased by children, touched, or overfed by guests will increase your pets stress level as well as your own.

Dr. Bradley Osgood of Brentwood Animal Hospital (Oak Creek, WI) highly suggests thinking carefully before adding your pet to the wedding list. If you are stressed, they will be stressed and act out for attention. Think of what is best for your pet (and for you) on your wedding day. Dr. Brad suggests pampering your pet with special attention leading up to the wedding to reaffirm them that while a change is present it will not affect your relationship with your fur baby. Silence the inner bridezilla, leave your four legged guest off the wedding list.

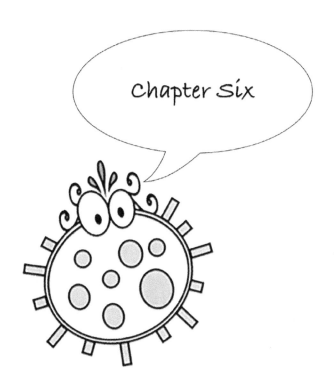

To theme or not to theme...
Decorating Dilemma's

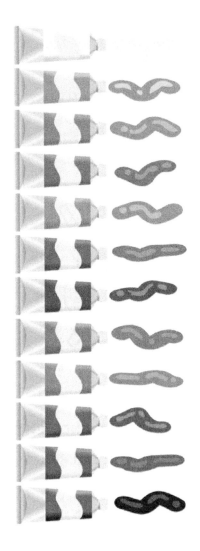

My Signature Colors are...

Choosing a color palette for your wedding celebration is not as easy as choosing your two favorite colors and making them the foundation for every wedding detail. A color palette is a reflection of you as a couple and sets the mood for the wedding celebration.

The color(s) of your wedding may be your favorite color from childhood, a current trend or theme. Don't be too quick to decide since there are several things to consider before you set your wedding colors in stone.

- Consider your venue
  - The venue will certainly play a key role with wedding colors. Trying to cover up or distract from the venue colors to coordinate with the wedding colors is a costly endeavor.
- The time of year
  - Just like your wardrobe, the season can influence your wedding color palette. Pastels look better in spring while dark tones are better suited for fall. There are no exact "rules" for this but it will be easier to find items in the given season rather than out of season.
- Set the mood
  - Color sets the mood for a wedding as much as time of day, location, or time of year. If you prefer a more dramatic look, then the dark rich jewel tones would work better than pastels.

It is very easy to get caught up in only considering the exact wedding color(s). The bridezilla virus appears when the bride has to have to match the exact color for everything. Think of your wedding planning in terms of style, formality, texture, and mood rather than color.

Matchy - Matchy

Imagine a white plate filled with white rice, mash potatoes, and fish covered with a white sauce. Now step back from the table, change the lighting of the room and what do you see on the plate? Chances are it is very difficult to distinguish each of the elements separately since they are all the same color. This is what happens when the bridezilla virus infects the bride with the "matchy - matchy" strain of the disease.

According to Wikipedia, matchy - matchy is an adjective used to describe something or someone that is very or excessively color coordinated. In the world of wedding planning, matchy – matchy occurs when the bride has to have a perfectly color match for everything including the invitations, wedding accessories, bridesmaid's dresses, flowers, and the table linens. There is no variance in color and everything will appear dull. The bridezilla virus affects not only the bride but anyone assisting the bride who is trying to find an exact color match. Virus symptoms include major disappointment, frustration, sleepless nights, and countless hours of searching the internet or traveling around town like a scavenger hunt.

In order to keep the matchy - matchy strain of the bridezilla virus from ruining your life, choose a palette of colors rather than one single color. Various shades of a color create interest gives the bride new options for the wedding celebration. Complementary colors (colors directly opposite each other in the color spectrum) or metallic (gold, silver, copper) add interest and will enhance any item.

If you choose to have a matchy – matchy wedding, try to create interest with texture and light for a new twist. Just be flexible to accept subtle variances in color. Different companies use various dye lots to produce their merchandise. Do not let the bridezilla virus ruin your wedding if you do not get the exact wedding color you selected. I guarantee no one will notice except you.

Sliding Scale

You found a centerpiece style you love. You purchased the components and created your masterpiece. At home the centerpiece looks amazing and you are so proud of your accomplishment. Once delivered to the venue and placed on the dining table, it lost among a sea of dinnerware. Your un-noticed centerpiece is suffering from S-2-S (size to scale) syndrome. Size to scale syndrome will cause the bridezilla virus to surface when you realize that your centerpiece vision will not be materialized. How do you suppress the bridezilla virus from surfacing? By following a few simple rules of design, you will be able to create decorations that "fit" your space.

A few questions you should ask yourself before deciding on decorating your venue(s) are:

- How long will we be using the venue space?
- How large is the venue space?
  - Room size
  - Ceiling height
    - Notice if there are hanging lights, beams, or chandeliers

- Flooring type
- Table size

To determine the height of an arrangement, it is best to take the height of the room and divide by 3. The simple rule of thirds visually helps to determine balance.

Example:

If you have a ceiling height of 15′ with 3′ hanging chandeliers your height of the room is decreased by 3′ bring your room height to 12′. Next divide the new room height by 3 which equal 4′ sections.

To determine the height of the centerpiece, take the 4′ section and times by 2. The ideal height of the decorations should be about 8′ including your table.

Here comes the fun part... you can either bring the ceiling height down (by hanging decorations from the ceiling or chandeliers with prior approval) or extending the height of the centerpiece to reach your ideal height.

To determine the height of a centerpiece, take your "ideal" height; subtract the height of the table and the height of the vase. This will give you an approximate size a centerpiece should be.

An ideal height of 8′ = 96 inches, Table height = 30 inches, in theory the centerpiece height ideally should be 66″ from table to top of the highest point. This is why branches are widely used to extend the height of a centerpiece to achieve the "ideal" size.

This may seem to be an unrealistic number but keep in mind you need to look at the décor and colors of the room. Color affects the feeling of the room and the impending decorations. Darker colors create a feeling of weight, while lighter colors create a more spacious feeling. If you use darker or brighter colors, a lower centerpiece will create the visual weight needed to balance the room.

One must also consider the width of the arrangement or centerpiece needed. The size and type of the table and the size of the place setting will determine the available space available for the centerpiece.

A typical place setting is approximately 18″ wide and 15″ deep (table edge to center of table.) Do not forget to add the table essentials – salt, pepper, bread baskets, etc. to the table setting. This may sound a bit confusing but nothing can bring out the bridezilla virus for you and your guests faster than having you dream centerpiece to too big or too small for your table.

To determine the available space for your table centerpiece and all other accessories (candles, favors, table numbers, and pictures) you may follow the chart.

- 72" round table (seats 8-10) – 24" available space
- 60" round table (seats 6-8) – 20" available space
- 48" round table (seats 4-6) – 18" available space
- 6' / 8' long tables (tables are 30" wide) – no available space without invading the place setting

One last consideration in determining the correct size of your centerpiece is the distraction factor. The most beautiful centerpiece in the world will be considered unacceptable if your guests are unable to see the guests seated at the opposite end of the table. Many guests will remove the floral arrangement it is in their way. To avoid this from happening, keep in mind that centerpieces should be no higher than 14 inches for a lower arrangement. For a tall arrangement the flowers should begin at 22 inches to avoid interruption of eye contact between guests.

When in doubt, create or purchase a sample centerpiece and bring it to the venue. Try it out and see if it works for your vision. This way you are able to make any adjustments prior to the wedding day. This is the best way to keep the bridezilla virus from surfacing.

ALWAYS ask the venue before installing any decorations. Discuss with them your plans including set-up, break-down, and disposal. NEVER assume you are able to use nails, tape or glue in the venue without written consent. Even with written consent, spell out your decorating plans in detail to avoid any disappointment, legal action, or cleaning fee. This is one time that it is not better to ask for forgiveness, you must get permission.

Don't Get Poked

I LOVE PINTEREST! I can search for hours in various areas of interest and never be bored. There is a plethora of information that I never knew existed. To a bride, Pinterest is the DIY life saver to have a beautiful wedding on a budget. Pinterest offers a couple hundreds, if not thousands of wedding ideas. If used properly, Pinterest can be very useful tool with wedding planning and yet it can be a bride, in addition to, a vendor's worst nightmare.

Problems arise when a bride has unreasonable expectations for their wedding from ideas pinned from Pinterest. Unfortunately, many brides are unable to grasp the fact that not everyone is able to create the items posted on Pinterest. To the average crafter with unlimited time or financial restraints, the craft or project may be attempted several times with revisions until the craft or project is similar to the picture shown. To the budget conscious bride with limited time and finances, the outcome of the attempted craft or project may not be as shown, take ten times the amount of time to construct, and costs more than purchasing the same item off Etsy or having a professional create it.

The best way not to get poked by Pinterest is to use the site as inspiration. Do not try to replicate the pins but take bits and pieces of favored pins and incorporate them into your celebration at the level of crafting ability at hand.

To use Pinterest effectively create one main public board and one main private board. This way you can pin favored items on your private board without criticism from others while using the public board for discussion. Remember a wedding is a public event while a marriage is private.

The best way to use Pinterest is to pin everything you would like for your wedding. Go wild and gather as many ideas as possible. Next, analyze your pins to find similarities. Create boards consisting of the similar pins. Start deleting unwanted pins to narrow your pins to your top picks. Stop pinning when decisions are made and orders are placed.

Remember....

Pinterest = Inspiration

DIY......LMAO!

With the introduction of the internet, the do it yourself bride was reborn. Thousands of ideas are literally at your fingertips twenty-four hours a day, seven days a week. Tutorials, pictures, and instructions give the novice crafter a new found sense of confidence with easy to follow instructions. Gone are the days of traveling all over town to purchase the needed materials to complete a project. Now materials are available from various sources with a click of a button and delivered right to your doorstep for a modest fee. What could possibly go wrong? In one word...everything!

The do it yourself (DIY) projects are a wonderful money saver. It is a way for the bride; her mother, friends, and other family members to showcase their talents. It can also be a costly lesson for those with limited time, talent, and experience to complete the chosen project. DIY projects, pictures, and instructions look beautiful when finished but may not be easy to complete. This may be very misleading to the untrained eye. It only takes the right composition, proper lighting, and a popular theme to leer the bride to buy items they may not need. There are a few exceptions to this and the outcome is a beautiful, money saving event but it does come at a cost.

The DIY bug usually bites early in the wedding planning process after the major decisions (venue, entertainment, dress, etc.) have been completed and there is nothing for the bride to do except wait for another planning milestone to appear. The compulsive act of continuously working on the wedding planning begins with DIY projects. It is like an addictive drug to some brides which may be perceived as a mild symptom of the bridezilla virus.

Creating your own projects is a way to customize your wedding celebration. With proper knowledge, the correct amount of construction time, practice, and a little patience great things can be accomplished.

A few things to consider when considering a DIY project are:

- The finished product rarely looks like the picture.
- Additional materials may be needed to enhance the finished product
- Frustration sets in when the final result is not what you envisioned
- Extraordinary time commitment to complete the projects
- One is doable, ten is bearable, thirty is insanity, and three hundred is just plain nuts.
- Storage requirements for finished projects
- Transportation and set up of finished projects
- Removal of finished projects
- Disposal of finished projects
- Finished products may cost more than purchasing them already finished

There is a rule to follow when attempting a DIY project for your wedding. If you can finish it months in advance and there is no time restraint, go for it. If it is a time-sensitive project or too large of a project to take on then do not risk it. The final days before your wedding are very hectic. The bride is very susceptible to catching the bridezilla virus at this time especially if there are unfinished projects to complete and the clock is ticking. Last minute errands, long lists of things to finish, entertaining out of town guests are just a few things to push a bride over the edge. Finishing a DIY project should not add to the stress of the wedding week.

There are five main items that should be left to professionals for a stressful free event:

1. Flowers

The construction of the personal flowers (bridal bouquet, bridesmaid bouquets, etc.) is more difficult and time consuming for the novice floral designer. Fresh flowers are perishable and need refrigeration along with proper hydration for the blooms to be developed for the wedding bouquets.

2. Your Hair

We are our own worst critic concerning our looks on your wedding day especially with hair styling. Attempting to do your own hair styling on the day of your wedding is time consuming and frustrating if your hair is not behaving. Even if you have practiced doing your hair style, your hair will do what it wants that day. Having a stylist do your hair is one way to tame the beast and pamper yourself on your wedding day.

3. Planning/Coordination

You have lists of exactly what you want; you have people in place to execute your plans, but who will ensure that everyone is in place? A wonderful event takes both proper planning and flawless execution. Since you are a bit busy that day, hire someone to run your event so you can relax and not let the bridezilla virus overcome your day and you can be stress free and present at your event.

4. Photography

The one way to remember your wedding day is through

actual photographs along with digital files. After the memories fade, flowers die, cake eaten, and the wedding is over only the photographs remain. Through photographs you relive, remember, and relive the moments of that day. A professional photographer understands composition, lighting, and their equipment. They are able to enhance, edit, and preserve your memories without bias. Family members with a cell phone or a point and shoot camera are capable to take a picture but a photographer captures a memory.

5. **Food**

Preparing a meal for two is different than preparing a meal for two hundred. Asking friends and family to prepare food for your wedding is asking for problems. You need to consider that friends and family are no longer guests at your wedding but now vendors. They are unable to enjoy the celebration since they will be working it. In addition, many venues require a professional caterer for health reasons. Do not be remembered for causing your wedding guests to be ill from eating food at your wedding or not eating at all since there wasn't enough to go around. Trust the professionals to deliver a delicious, well prepared meal.

DIY projects may save money and is a wonderful way of putting a personal touch to your wedding celebration. If you do not procrastinate and stick to a completion timeline on your projects, the bridezilla virus will lay dormant and you will be stress free. Know your limitations and accept it is ok to have someone do it for you instead of doing it yourself.

Blooming Miracles

Flowers have been a part of the wedding celebration dating as far back to the ancient Greeks. At that time, flowers and plants were constructed into crowns (wreaths) and worn upon the heads of both the bride and groom much like the Caesar's laurels at a toga party. The crowns or garland bouquets were considered a gift of nature and a symbol of love and happiness. Often made of various herbs and bulbs of garlic, folklore rumored these herbs to have different meanings toward life and marriage. Garlic was used to ward off any evil spirits that might intervene in the ceremony or curse the couple's future together. Garlic combined with sage meant that the bride would gather great wisdom and learn goodness. Dill was considered the herb of lust. When with herb was combined with garlic, the bride would only lust for her husband. Over time, the herbs and garlic were replaced by fragrant blooms with each having a different meaning. Flowers to this day are used as a decorative touch to the wedding celebration. The widespread appeal, availability, and affordable prices

make flowers the most used decoration at a wedding. Each bride puts a different value on the
presence of flowers at their wedding. Some brides feel they are not necessary while others cannot have enough adorn her, the ceremony venue, and the reception.

Deciding on the type of flowers is as important as the person who will design them. Some brides decide to hire their sister's girlfriend neighbor's cousin who constructs bouquets in their garage instead of a professional floral designer to save money. Problems arise when your sister's girlfriend neighbor's cousin is unable to fulfill the floral vision. The bridezilla virus grows in intensity and blooms with a fragrance that is not very pleasant when flowers are not at the wedding as promised. Unfortunately, this scenario occurs quite often. Hiring someone other than a professional floral designer to save money is not always the best option. In the long run you land up spending more than you save.

Professional florists have the ability to obtain the freshest flowers from local floral wholesalers/growers to create your wedding flowers. In addition, the professional florists have the knowledge, training, experience, refrigeration, supplies, and delivery vehicles. Additional personnel are available from your professional florist if needed to design, create, transport, set-up, take-down, and provide peace of mind.

With the creation of Pinterest, brides have unlimited floral suggestions to decorate their wedding. This is both a blessing and a curse. On one hand, the possibilities are endless and floral designs range from frugal to extravagant. On the other hand, too many possibilities cause confusion, false hope, and disappointment when the expectations are unobtainable.

The bridezilla virus begins to bloom when the bride sees it, wants it, and it is not available. Just because you see it on the internet doesn't mean it is real. Computer enhancement programs alter and adjust colors in a digital file to create an illusion. Computer monitors vary in color settings which gives a misrepresentation of the actual flower. While the flowers are beautiful on the web, most flower colors are not as vibrant in

nature and this leads many brides to be disappointed and the bridezilla virus continues to develop.

Fresh flowers are a wonderful addition to a wedding celebration. Special considerations should be made when purchasing fresh flowers.

Keep in mind the following:

- Type of flowers
  - Certain flowers have a strong fragrance that could trigger allergies. Swollen itchy eyes, runny nose, sinus pressure, headaches and a sore throat are not wanted symptoms for your wedding day.
- Seasonal availability
  - Certain flowers are only available during specific seasons. Limited availability may be available from Holland, South America, or California but they come at a cost.
- Perishable
  - Fresh flowers are perishable and not meant to live forever.

Wedding flowers are divided into three main categories-personal, ceremony and reception.

- **Personal flowers** are any flower(s) presented to a person to carry, wear, or toss which include the Bridal bouquet, bridesmaid(s) bouquets, flower girl flowers, gentlemen boutonnieres/buttonholes, and corsages.
- **Ceremony flowers** are any flowers or plants used to enhance the ceremony location which include the Wedding Arch, Chuppah, altar bouquets, aisle chair/pew décor, candelabra, religious gifts/ceremonies, and aisle decoration.
- **Reception flowers** include table centerpieces, head table decoration, guest book adornment, place card & gift table flowers, cake top, and cake table flowers.

The flowers the bride chooses to carry for her wedding day becomes a reflection of her: unique, beautiful, elegant, and sometimes even colorful. Several considerations must be addressed when ordering personal flowers. The style of bouquet should complement and not detract from the wedding gown and the bride herself. In addition, the larger the bouquet, the heavier the bouquet is to carry. Imagine carrying a gallon of milk all day, your arms will be aching, you will be cranky, and everyone will assume you have been infected by the bridezilla virus.

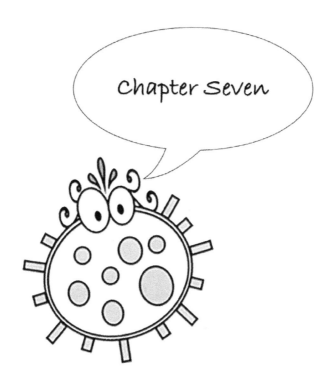

Tiers of Joy

Piece of Cake

The crowning jewel of the wedding celebration (besides the happy couple) is the cake! The wedding cake has been a part of the wedding celebration for centuries.

One of the sweetest tasks to accomplish is wedding cake shopping. Cake shopping is not for the faint of heart. It requires a base layer of food to absorb the sugar, something to cleanse the pallet between varieties, and of course.... stretchy pants! One may think that the bridezilla virus would not be present during this "sweet" event but this is untrue. The bridezilla virus thrives on sugar, caffeine, and lack of sleep.

Before you dive in and make appointments:

- Have a guest count to determine size of cake needed
- Bring examples of wedding cake styles you prefer
- Make a list of cake flavors you are interested in

- Bring examples of wedding cake decoration ideas
- Bring any accessories you would like incorporated with the cake
- Be open to suggestions and let your baker mix up some magic!

Debbie Pagel of Eat Cake! (Milwaukee, WI) highly suggests ordering a piece of cake for each guest attending the wedding. Cutting the budget by not ordering enough cake will only cause issues. Everyone cuts cake in a different way. In addition, if the wedding cake is being served, the wait staff will serve a piece of cake to each place setting even if no one is present. Caterers will panic if there is not enough cake to go around so please avoid having the bridezilla virus affect your caterer and wait staff, order enough cake. If you happen to have some left over wedding cake…. score!

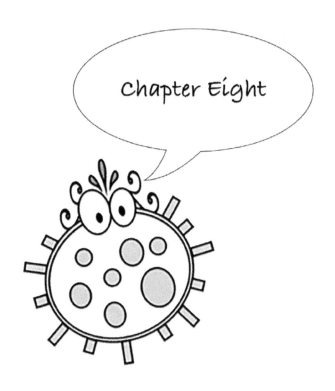

Chapter Eight

Just Shoot Me!

Freeze Frame

It was once said that a picture is worth a thousand words, well I feel it is worth a lifetime of memories. A photograph captures a special moment in time, preserving it for generations. Wedding photos document history, capture trends, and comic poses of drunken family and friends.

Hiring a photographer to capture your wedding memories should not be taken lightly. You are hiring the photographer's creative expression, talent, knowledge, and personality. This is the person who will document your wedding. You will have your memories (from your perspective) of your special day. Your photographer will show you everything you may have missed.

The bridezilla virus may not surface until you see the proofs of the wedding day. To ensure that the virus does not show up on your photographs there are several precautionary steps you can take to nip the virus in the bud.

- On your wedding day do not try to act like a supermodel.
- Un-natural poses may be awkward and unflattering.
- Do not have unrealistic expectations; trust your photographer to bring you best side forward.
- Another area of concern may be your coloring. An un-natural orange glow from a bottle or tanning bed may make you look like an alien from your favorite movie. Photoshop can help soften this look but it is a costly process.

Your wedding day will be over in a flash, make sure your camera phone enthusiasts do not get in the way of your photographer. You have limited time to get the photos in the available light. Camera phone photo enthusiasts make your photographer's job difficult and sometimes impossible. Allow your photo enthusiasts a special photo session when your photographer is finished (time allowing.)

Keep in mind that the camera will pick up any tension or document family drama through their body language. Try to keep bickering family members apart especially when being photographed. No family is perfect. In order to have a picture "perfect" day, ask your family members to express the joy they have for you on your special day and leave behind any ill will for each other...just for today. Do not let the bridezilla virus surface if your family members do not comply. Take a deep breath and enjoy the day. You can always Photoshop them out! (just kidding.)

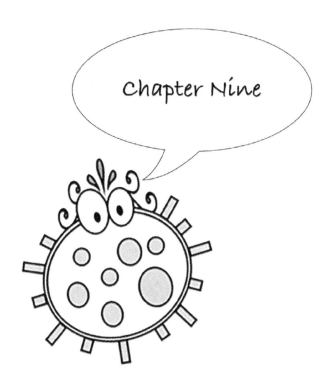

Juggling Act...

Musical Chairs

As the RSVP's begin to arrive, it is time to consider a seating chart for your celebration. A seating chart can help avoid confusion, potential guest seating issues, and overall guest experience.

While you want every guest to feel welcome and comfortable, preparing the seating chart is often the worst challenge a couple must complete prior to the wedding. It is a frustrating and unforgiving job with someone tending to be unhappy with the arrangements. A seating chart is an excellent way of avoiding uninvited guests to "pop" in for a free meal. In addition, a seating chart may also inform you who did not show up for the celebration.

A seating chart is a game of musical chairs. This is one area where the bridezilla virus is anxiously waiting to play this game and win. A seating chart is a task that needs to be started sooner rather than later. Completing a seating cart on the morning of the wedding or a few days before will cause the bridezilla virus to emerge, stay, and show its ugly face throughout the rest of your wedding celebration.

With the electronic age, there are many seating chart apps and free websites to make the seating chart process much easier to complete. If this is not an option, create a spreadsheet with several columns. Place your guest list in one column and by relationship (meaning if they are a friend or family) in another. You may even have another column with additional notes if there are any issues between guests who should not be seated next to each other. Your venue should be able to provide and a basic chart of proposed floor plan along with the type, size, and seating capacity for your event. This will serve as your guide to playing musical chairs.

Once the RSVP's arrive immediately begin assigning guests to tables. Move the guests around until you feel comfortable with the results and voila it's done. It is best to accept any family advice without issue while completing a seating chart. Your family may know of any underlying issues which may cause some guests to feel uncomfortable with whom they are seated with.

There is no right or wrong way to prepare a seating chart but there are several mishaps that can occur. Several things will help keep the bridezilla virus dormant:

- Do not seat some of the parents at the bridal table unless you can seat all-including stepparents
- Do assign guests to table where they know someone
- Do not seat all of your guests with only people they've met before.
- Do not play matchmaker with your single guests.
- Do consider your guest's personalities and interests while assigning tables.

Guests attending your wedding are happy to be a part of your wedding celebration. Do not over think the seating chart. Guests will only be sitting at their dinner tables for a maximum of ninety minutes. In the scheme of things is not a long time but can feel like an eternity being seated with individuals that do not get along.

Plus, one?

Unfortunately, there will be people who do not return their RSVP on time. You have deadlines to meet for the venue, caterer, florist, and the bridezilla virus is starting to get you enraged. You have a timeline to follow and your guests are not following through with their responses. You could send a reminder email to the lax responders but the best (and fastest) way to get an answer is simply to call and ask their intentions.

The RSVP's are rolling in and suddenly you noticed that your guests are including a plus one or children that were not listed on the invitation. Most times to avoid confrontation and hurt feelings, nothing is said to the invited guest. An unexpected guest can be a costly addition. In addition to the cost of the meal, added tables may be needed which adds table cloths, chair covers, and centerpieces. You also run the risk of going over capacity at the venue causing other to be uncomfortable in a more restrictive space. The bridezilla virus is lurking in the shadows waiting to appear when the time is right. Keep the virus dormant by taking control of the situation and not yielding to added costs that could be avoided.

How to handle such a situation? The best way to handle this situation is to call personally rather than waiting for an email that may not be seen or answered. Explain that you are thrilled that they can attend your celebration. State you are sorry for any misunderstanding but the invitation was only for them. Be firm but understanding. State again that the two of you hope that they will still be able to come to the celebration and thank for their understanding.

When children are included on the RVSP and it is an adult only affair....

Remind guests that you want them to enjoy your celebration. Watching a small child in a hectic, stressful situation is difficult and time consuming. Parents are unable to fully enjoy the celebration since parenting trumps the wedding. Neglectful/pre-occupied parent unknowingly create a stressful environment for your guests when a child begins to act up. Not everyone understands that a child may be restless, loud, or misbehave in this type of setting. This may not always apply to older children that can be entertained with an electronic device. Older pre-occupied children are easier to manage but still may be an issue due to venue limitations.

If you allow one guest to bring a child, other guests with children will be upset that their child/children were not invited. Allowing a guest to bully you into agreeing to allow a child to attend can get out of hand very quickly. Your ballroom may quickly turn into a romper room if you are not careful. To avoid the bridezilla virus from surfacing at the wedding:

- Allow only one person to deal with the "children" issue. By having more than one person involve and lead to miscommunication and your worst nightmare may come true.
- Be sure to explicitly state in your invitations your views on having children being present or not being present at your event. Your guests may try to find a loop hole to squeeze their children into attending.

- Be aware that if a guest threatens not to come, the rudeness is theirs and not yours.

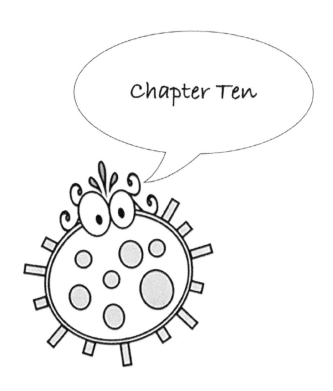

Chapter Ten

Dealing with your Mother

Mama-saurus...WRECKS!

How do you tell the woman who gave birth to you or raised you that she is driving you crazy? You love her but there are times throughout the wedding planning process that it is all about her. Planning a wedding can create a wonderful bonding experience, but it can also bring on added stress to the mother-daughter relationship. We are programmed from birth to respect our mothers and not to openly question her decisions. Unknowingly, mothers become infected by "wedding-perfection-itis" and turns into a Mama-saurus who can wreck your wedding.

There are many variations or types of the Mama-saurus: the vicarious, the critical, the emotional, the angry, and the controlling. The most dangerous of all the Mama-saurus types is the controlling variety. A mother with controlling tendencies tries to plan her daughter's wedding as if it was her wedding. These moms try to fit their daughter's weddings in a certain mold of what they always wanted while paying no attention of the wants or needs of the wedding couple.

Signs your mother is turning or has turned into a controlling mamasaurus are:

- **Makes you doubt yourself**
  - Since childhood she makes you feel like you are a child. Nothing you do will ever be right. Decisions you make are wrong if you did not consult her.
- **Psychotic stalking**
  - She needs to know where you are at all times. She is nosy and will cyber stalk you.
- **Controlling relationships and friends**
  - She will dominate conversations and eaves drop on others conversations to dominate them as well.
- **Guilt trips you**
  - She will whine on how little time you are spending with her and then talk in a small, weak, worn voice to show how she is suffering. If you stand your ground she will send you multiple text messages, emails, or phone calls with words to make you feel guilty for having an opinion.
- **Lies, belittles, condemning, and abuses you**
  - She is a proficient liar and mastered how to rally others to believe her web of deceit. Anyone who gives her an audience will receive an Oscar winning performance. She will always have a scowl on her face and manages to isolate you from your friends. She is first to point out your weaknesses and will embarrass you every chance she gets.
- **Gives you gifts with strings-attached**
  - She will graciously give you a gift and then use this gesture to make you do things for her. She will bring up things she has done for you and make you feel

obligated to return the favor.

- **Competes for yours and everyone's attention**
  - ○ She will drive your friends away so you are solely dependent on her. It is a form of isolation that puts her above everything else in your life.

The Mama-saurus inadvertently may wreck your wedding planning unless you take steps to control the beast. This is a difficult task to accomplish since the various versions of the Mama-saurus each have their own unique characteristics.

In the mind of Mama-saurus she will believe that if you take her advice, allow or accept a change she implicated, it now gives her free reign to alter your wedding plans to her liking. The Mama-saurus will deny this statement or claim the change is for your own good or this is the way it should be. If you allow this to happen, you just lost control of your wedding.

So, what is the best way to get back control of your wedding and your life without causing your mother pain and anguish? First, step back and understand that your mother/mother in law has emotions, feelings, and dreams about the milestones in your life including your wedding. Feelings of anxiety and abandonment may appear in your mother/mother in law as the wedding day approaches.

Moms want your day to be special so they may lose their cool when plans change without consultation. Being a mom never ends but it is not an excuse to have bad behavior even if they feel that it is in your best interest.

Be firm in your wedding vision but do make your mother/mother in law feel included in your day. Make a list of the no-compromise details that you and your fiancé are not

willing to have changed. Even if your mother/mother in law is paying for the wedding it does not give them the right to change anything without your approval. If there is opposition on this, you may have to graciously decline a monetary gift and pay for your wedding cerebration yourself. Do give your mom a task that isn't as important to you to such as a bridesmaid's luncheon, farewell brunch, welcome bag construction, or gift opening to plan. It will keep her distracted from meddling in the larger planning process. Sneaky.... yes, effective... ABSOLUTELY!

The most difficult conversation to have is when you tell your mother she is overstepping her bounds. The best is to address this as soon as signs are evident rather than waiting where bitter feelings may develop at a later stage and carry on for years. Keep calm when you confront her and explain how you feel. She may not even realize that she is upsetting you.

It is <u>NOT</u> Mother's Day ....
it's my wedding!

The wedding day has finally arrived and all the preparation, planning, and painful details have been laid out for the day when the coordinator can to take control and orchestrate your special day. So far you have managed to elude the bridezilla virus and you are in the home stretch. Suddenly, out of nowhere your mother is affected with a strain of the bridezilla virus! Different from being a mama-sauraus, your mom begins to feel it is her day and she is in charge. Your mother not only steps in as the hostess of the event but will be a real "mother" over situations. Moms will exert their motherly advice to everyone especially the bride. Your wedding day has now become "Mother's Day."

A wedding is an emotional time for the mothers of the wedding couple. Somehow on this day above all others, your mother sees you as a child playing dress up and not the woman standing before her getting married. Bad behavior from your mother may be her way of coping with the changes in her life. It is difficult to accept that her little girl is grown up

and even though you may be eighteen, thirty, or even fifty. This type of denial causes the "mothering" instinct to emerge. When she still considers you a child, she still believes it is up to her to call the shots and be the center of attention.

How do you gently remind your mother that it is not Mother's Day? This is tricky since you want everyone to enjoy the day without drama. The only way to accomplish this is to use a diversion with reverse psychology. On your wedding day do something special for your mom. Write her a letter thanking her for being your mom and teaching you about life. Explain that without her you would not a confident woman ready to begin this new adventure of marriage. Remind her you need her for advice and help when solicited since marriage can be challenging. Now, you may want to present her with a small gift (just between you girls) as a reminder how much she means to you. I guarantee if you do this, it will touch her heart and this specialized strain of the bridezilla virus will disappear. Now you can direct her to her responsibilities of the day and remind her to enjoy herself and be present at the wedding and not host it. Sneaky but it is 100% effective.

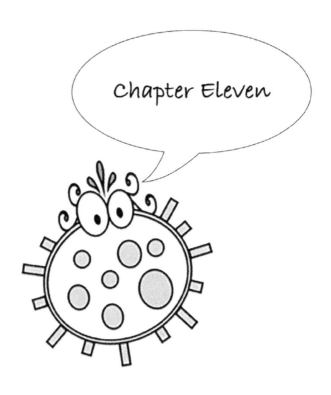

Melodramatic Meltdown

"Weather" it's nice or not

You have spent months, maybe even years, planning your wedding. Every detail is orchestrated to precision and then the weather forecast is for rain, extreme heat/cold, snow, hurricane, typhoon, or a tornado. This was not in your bridal plan or even considered to be an option for your wedding day. How dare the weather be anything but perfect on your special day!

Let's face it, bad or unfavorable weather is rotten any day of the year. When inclement weather is expected on the wedding day, the bridezilla virus surfaces with gale force winds and the bride is difficult to handle. Brides want to look their best on the wedding day. Bad weather makes a bride's mind runs wild with the worst possible scenarios from her

dress getting ruined to her hair style falling. Inclement weather can change the once mild matter bride to become unreasonable, inconsolable, and unhappy on her wedding day.

While planning your wedding, it is best to have an alternate plan or plans in place with a separate person in charge to implement a change or changes if necessary. Then accept that no one cannot control nature and move on. Inclement weather can be a blessing in disguise.

Many folklore legends believe that rain on your wedding day is a sign of good fortune and fertility. It may also signify unity in the respect that you are "tying the knot." Since a wet knot is harder the pull apart than a dry one, water creates a stronger bond. The Italian wedding saying "Sposa Bagnata,Sposa Fortunata" when translates to "Wet Bride, Lucky Bride" must be true!

Rain on your wedding day, besides being annoying, may be the best thing ever. The weather forecast may not be as you planned but your photographs will be amazing. A cloudy or gray tone day enables vibrant colors to be captured. A gray day does not create shadows to worry about and it creates a romantic setting for your photographs. Rain has healing qualities to relieve seasonal allergies and may give a temporary relief from airborne pollen.

Whatever the weather may be on your wedding day, it is uncontrollable. Do not let the bridezilla virus dampen your wedding day. Grab an umbrella, snow boots, sunscreen, or bug spray, move to plan B and enjoy the celebration.

It's my wedding...
(And I will cry if I want to)

The wedding is only a few weeks away. While you are clutching your planning binder it happens...the meltdown. A rollercoaster of emotions surface planning a wedding so it is natural for an incident to occur. How we handle to these "breakdowns" will determine if the bridezilla virus will surface or lay dormant.

Planning a wedding is not an easy task. It is a time- consuming endeavor in which professionals are paid to produce an exceptional event while most brides are focused with school or a career and have little time to devote to planning. The bridezilla virus symptoms first appear in the form of sleep and food deprivation. While trying to plan a wedding, brides neglect the basics of life. Some feel that the lack of food helps with dieting, while many feel the lack of sleep will be made up after the wedding. Brides turn ugly, snippy, and mean without food and/or sleep. While lack of food and/or sleep changes our personality, it does not give

you the right to be rude, mean, or disrespectful. Meltdowns appear when the bride feels misunderstood and alone.

Meltdowns take various forms and range in intensity. It is alright to have a meltdown but not to be melodramatic. There are options to control the meltdown and to control the bridezilla virus from developing. Use any of all of the following to get through your meltdown.

- **Cry** – A good cry is a wonderful physiological stress relieving option. Crying is not a sign of weakness but it feels good to get it all out.
- **Walk away** – When you are unable to be rational in your thinking or actions it is best to walk away, calm down, and gain clarity of the situation. Saying or doing anything in anger or a distressed state will end up in regret. Others will understand If you need a moment to collect your thoughts.
- **Find the root of the problem** – When a meltdown is beginning it is most often over some small detail that triggers the real hidden issue. Finding the root of the problem will eliminate future outbreaks.
- **Don't procrastinate** - Deal with issues as soon as you can. Letting things pile up can snowball and cause stress and the bridezilla virus to appear.
- **Don't hold on to problems that have been fixed.** Bringing up old problems that have been rectified will just get your upset. Best to let it go.

It is best to accept that a meltdown will happen to every bride during the wedding planning process. Once you recognize that a meltdown has begun, let it run its course. A sense of relief will overcome you as soon as your meltdown is over. Sometimes you just need to let go to gain control back in your life.

It's not what I thought
it would feel like.

Your wedding is an important day in your life. Many have been planning for this day for months, years, or even decades. Throughout the planning process, mixed emotions will emerge. Some emotions are of excitement and joy while others are of anger and disappointment. Envy even sneaks in an appearance from time to time. But which emotion is the correct one for a bride to feel? One thing for sure is no two people are the same and everyone will have their own experience. There is no right or wrong way to feel before, during, or after your wedding. Hopefully your wedding planning experience is a happy one without the bridezilla virus surfacing. It is best not to listen to anyone telling you how to feel. Trust in yourself and be present for the moment.

A wedding is a special commitment between two people. The love in your heart for the person you are committing yourself to is the one main emotion you should focus on.

You're backing out??

A good vendor is the key to a successful event. The relationship you develop with your vendor is a special one. These are the people who will bring your dreams into reality. After countless meetings you finally found the person or company you want to be part of your special day. Suddenly, you get a call that your chosen vendor has decided not to be a part of your celebration. You have no idea why they would not want your business. Well.... I can sum it up in two words: bridezilla virus.

If a vendor cancels an event, it means you have been affected by the bridezilla virus. Sadly, the bridezilla virus outbreak occurred without notice. Vendors do not cancel an event unless they feel it is unlikely for them to perform the service you requested. This decision may have been determined due to any of the following actions from the wedding couple:

- Unable to make a decision
- Changing you mind on a continuous basis
- Adding to your order and not accepting the added cost
- Too many emails, phone calls, or instant messages over non-relative issues
- Wedding couple being demanding
- Family members (mostly mothers) being demanding
- Unrealistic expectations
- Unfavorable reviews
- Lack of respect and/or manners

When a vendor backs out of your event, it does create a hiccup in wedding planning. They have a reason and you must respect their decision. No vendor wants to lose business but sometimes it is necessary to avoid future conflict, negative reviews, or failure to receive payment on services rendered.

Before moving forward to pick up the pieces of your broken wedding planning, you must look within yourself to find the bridezilla virus. Unless you suppress the virus, additional vendors may follow suit and cancel as well. No one wants to be known as a "B."

To be sure your vendors will not dessert you on your wedding day be open to their suggestions. Accept what is and not what could be. Negotiate within reason and remember that vendors are people too and deserve respect. These talented individuals want your event to be spectacular. Learn to keep the bridezilla virus under control and have a memorable event.

What If....

"What if" are two simple words that when put together can cause fear in anyone but especially in brides. What if my make-up runs and I look like a raccoon? What if my dress doesn't fit? What if no one shows up? What if I trip walking down the aisle? What if I get a zit? (Don't use Windex!) These and more inner fears have plagued brides for centuries. Obsessing over one or any "what if" can cause the bridezilla virus to emerge, grow, and flourish.

When "what if" happens always move to plan B whatever that may be. You may fall- but someone will pick you up. Your dress may not fit perfectly- but that is what safety pins and duct tape is for. Your cake may not show up or be dropped- so a fast run to donut store may fill the bill. If your makeup runs and you look like a raccoon, chances are everyone else looks the same. Something will happen on your wedding day, it is inevitable.

How do you make a bride stop saying "what if" and accept "what is?" The answer is to get vaccinated against the bridezilla virus by conquering your fears and learn how to stop worrying about the unknown. This is easier to accomplish than you may think. The simple solution is to

accept that something will go wrong. Real life is a far cry from the movies or photographs that have been edited to perfection. When something doesn't go as planned those magical mishaps become memories we embrace and cherish. The bridal duties on your wedding day include being a gracious host and enjoying the festivities. Stop worrying about little missed details and be present on the day you spent a good part of a year planning. This means put away your cell phone!

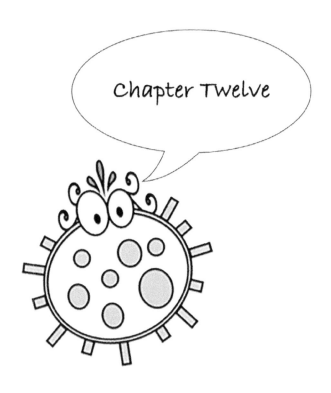

Chapter Twelve

Shocking Discoveries

Sticker Shock

It's a painful time in every bride's life...to pay the wedding bills. Paying bills is an awful task especially when you have saved for your wedding day and you reached your goal. It's just nice to see a lump sum in one place even if it is for a short time! Once the bills are totaled, the deposits or retainers are deducted, and the remaining balance is more than you ever imagined...you are experiencing sticker shock.

If you had the discipline to keep to your budgeted amount and did not add or change your original orders with your vendors, you should be fine. Chances are this did not happen. There is always something to add to a wedding celebration.

Weddings are based on emotion. We all want to create the fairy tale and with the help of Pinterest, advice from friends/family, and the internet it can be done but it comes at a cost.

Once a couple has secured the key elements and the preliminary estimates are in place, a false set of reliefs bestows the couple that they are on or under budget. At this point, a small addition here, a small change there seems innocent

enough and affordable until the numbers are tallied. Nothing can push a couple over the edge than money issues

especially when it involves a wedding. The bridezilla virus is just waiting patiently to affect the happy couple and cause havoc.

What do you do? Cry? Scream? Borrow money? Cancel all additions? These are all options but the best thing to do is to stop, breathe, and work as a couple to come up with a solution. Communicate honestly to your vendors and each other. Acting hastily will cause issues and tension between the couple and will allow the bridezilla virus to emerge.

Best to examine your wedding additions, the over budget amount, and signed contracts to see how to proceed to get your budget back under control. Keep focused, accept the outcome of your decisions, and do not focus on what could have been.

Shooting Yourself with bullet points!

There are proven facts that planning a wedding can be stressful. Even the most organized person will have a disorganized moment or two, three, or four. With a multitude of wedding planners, daily planners, and hundreds of available planning apps, it is extremely easy to get caught up in planning details. Lists upon lists with bullet points will appear on post-it notes in random places. Brides begin to get overwhelmed causing most to be a bit scatterbrained. The symptoms seem to increase as the wedding day approaches.

Sometimes, you can shoot yourself with too many bullet points. But when is it enough? When are there too many lists? The simple answer to this question is when you try to micromanage the entire event.

How do you dodge the bullet points? Ask for help. Condense the wedding planner; trust in your vendors, and start prepping with your day of coordinator at least 4 weeks prior to the event. Do create a mini version of your wedding plan. Include the key people, contact phone numbers (with alternate phone numbers too,) delivery times, and any remarks of that vendor.

It does not make you a failure to ask for help. You are planning one of life's most memorable events. The bridezilla virus emerges when you try to do it all. Don't let the bridezilla virus ruin your event; delegate, eliminate, and articulate.

"Bin" there

Preparing for your wedding day requires the acquisition of a lot of items. From personal items to centerpieces and everything in between, items are gathered, stored, and usually kept in the bag/box they came in until the wedding day. Then they are brought to the ceremony or reception, opened, used and tossed in some other box with the original packaging in some other bag/box. The disorganized mess is left to clean up at the end of the night and sort out days after the event. The answer to calm your chaos is simple- storage tote or what I to call "bins."

Storage totes or bins are available in various sizes and materials. I suggest purchasing plastic ones with an attached hinged cover if possible. It is much easier to have an attached top rather than trying to find the top amongst the mess. If hinged totes are not available, any style or type will do. Plastic bins are reusable, most often water-proof, and stackable.

Organization is the best defense against the bridezilla virus. Bins are a bride's best friends. To control the chaos and ward off the bridezilla virus on your wedding day here are a few helpful bin hints.

- Have large bins available for each bridesmaid, mothers, and yourself. Label each bin with each name and advise everyone that it is for ALL of their personal items. The pre wedding staging area will stay clutter free and there is a lesser chance of items getting lost or stolen. The bins can then be transferred to the reception location while the bridal party is off taking photos and celebrating the marriage.

- Keep packing material together for each item brought to the ceremony and reception. Separate boxes that are clearly marked with the items in the box will allow the clean-up crew to keep items organized and easily transportable.

- Create a master list of the bins along with who will be in charge of set-up and breakdown. A numbering system works well.

- Keep a separate smaller bin with items that can be reached easily to help the bride throughout the day. Items such as: several pair of shoes, breath mints, aspirin, medication, deodorant, tennis ball (for a fast foot massage), feminine hygiene products, etc.

- Have an emergency kit available for life's little mishaps.

- Bins should also be purchased to pack your wedding gifts for transport home.

Purchasing bins is an additional cost that may seem excessive at the time but it will save you hours of looking for misplaced items and it will keep you organized and virus free.

Another very important investment is a folding cart. This ($50-$70) investment is a life and time saver. Why walk twice as much? Pull it!

Chapter Thirteen

The Final Countdown

What was that?

Throughout the wedding planning process, many notice that the bride becomes forgetful. This is simply not a case of being over tired; it is a strain of the bridezilla virus. Bridal brain (also known as BB) is the temporary condition of forgetfulness. BB may lead to a full outbreak of the bridezilla virus if not diagnosed in the early stages. Bridal brain may even be the silent celebration killer.

With the stress of wedding planning, we overload our brain with details. Even the smallest detail is important to a bride. I believe the need to host a memorable event causes even the simplest of task to be forgotten. Early onset of bridal brain may be seen early in the wedding planning process.

Several areas where bridal brain prevails in the early stages of wedding planning are:

Not setting up in-person appointments. Doing preliminary research online is great, but a face-to-face meeting is necessary with vendors.

You need to know who you are working with and make sure you and your vendor are on the same page with your wants, needs, and expectations.

Not asking for referrals. Be sure to read online reviews about your vendors. Do check the Better Business Bureau for any possible complaints. Talks to people that have worked with the vendor.

- **Not reading the fine print.** <u>Always</u> read any contract carefully, especially when doing business online. In addition, read the return policy to make sure you get all of your money back if there is a problem with the order (damaged, lost, late, wrong item, quality.)

- **Not requesting samples.** Never accept a color online, ask for a sample to be positive that it is correct.

- **Not keeping a paper trail.** Keep all email correspondence with vendors in a safe place. Print hard copies for your files. Always keep any correspondences for proof of what you agreed on to avoid the bridezilla virus occurring on your wedding day. Save every receipt and original packing material for easy returns if need be.

- **Not keeping up with your wedding website.** This is your life line to avoid multiple phone calls asking about wedding day details, hotel availability, dress code, registry details and more.

A few weeks prior to the ceremony bridal brain syndrome intensifies. Several last minute items that are often forgotten are:

- **Thank you gifts**
    - A thank you gift is customary for the bridal party as a sign of appreciation

- ○ Favors for the wedding guests
- ○ Groom's gift
- ○ Parent's gift

- **Wrapping gifts**

- **Vendor meals**
  - ○ It is necessary to feed your vendors (band members, DJ, photographer, videographer, any assistants)

- **Marriage license**
  - ○ Your wedding is not legal without a license. Be sure to have the necessary documents to receive the license in a timely manner.
  - ○ Put the marriage license in a safe place and send yourself an email reminding you where it is.

On your wedding day, the bridal brain virus will bloom into the bridezilla virus if you forget the following:

Eat

- Brides are often too busy, filled with excitement, and often stressed. It is critical for the entire wedding party, especially the bride, to eat something to prevent hunger-related issues such as dizziness, fainting, and nausea. If you are too nervous to eat a meal, try a belly-friendly food like toast, oatmeal, pretzels, or cereal.

Use the rest room

- Before dressing, use the rest room. It may be silly to remind yourself but it is increasingly more difficult to use the rest room in your gown.
-

Put on a button-down shirt

- Getting your hair done, make applied, and when you are ready to put your gown on you cannot remove your top without undoing what was just done. If you do not look your best, the bridezilla virus will be unleashed.
-

Hydrate

- Just like eating, your body needs hydration to be 100%. If you are marrying in the summer months or in a tropical location, be hydrated is a necessary for a pleasant day.

After the vows have been said, rings exchanged, and you are married, there are a few things you should do first to save yourself sudden flashes of the bridezilla virus.

- Take several minutes with your partner to treasure the moment. Steal a kiss, hold each other, and be in the moment. This may be the only chance you get to be alone all day.
- Put your marriage license in a safe place.

Bridal brain will disappear when the stress of the day has subsided. Until it does, make lists to complete, and be patient this too will pass.

You need it? I got it!!

Being prepared for your wedding day or any special event is crucial to the happy bride, bridesmaid, or even wedding guest. An unhappy bride will contract the bridezilla virus and affect others if not caught in the incubation stage. Several wedding day survival kits will fit the prescription for a happy wedding experience. A parts organizer box (available from your local hardware or box store) works perfectly to house the individual components of your survival kit to make them easily accessible at a moment's notice. I would suggest creating several kits- bride, bridesmaids, groom, and parents. This way no one will have to hunt for the only kit available.

Some items to include in your kits are:

- Alcohol (if all else fails)
- Baby powder
- Blotting papers
- Breath mints or mouth wash

- Bug spray
- Cash
- Cell phone
- Cell phone charger
- Chap stick
- Cooling towel
- Curling iron/flat iron
- Dental floss
- Dental floss/toothpicks
- Deodorant
- Extension cord
- Extra earring backs
- Eye drops
- Feminine products
- Flash light/matches
- Hair brush/comb
- Hair clips, bobby pins
- Hair spray/ hair gel
- Hand lotion
- Hand sanitizer
- Iron or steamer
- Lighter
- Lint roller
- Make up- powder, blush, lip stick, cover up etc.
- Medicine (pain reliever, allergy, antacid)
- Mini first aid kit (band-aids, burn-relief, antiseptic gel)
- Mini sewing kit with scissors, needles, thread, buttons, and safety pins.
- Nail clipper
- Nail file
- Nail polish (clear and color you are wearing)
- Pen/ paper
- Phone numbers of all wedding participants
- Q-tips @ makeup remover
- Razor

- Saline solution
- Snacks-granola bar, protein bar
- Stain remover pen
- Static cling spray
- Straws
- Sunscreen
- Super Glue
- Tennis ball
- Tissues
- Tooth brush/tooth paste
- Towel-ettes or baby wipes
- Tweezers
- Umbrella
- Utility knife
- Water
- White chalk
- White duct tape or hem tape
- Wrinkle remover

Chapter Fourteen

Wedding Daze

Attitude with a Twist...

You may verbally state during the wedding planning process or even on the wedding day that everything is fine but your body may be saying something different. Deciphering a person's body language has been recognized and documented dating back to 1605. Body language is the nonverbal expression of your feelings. UCLA research has shown that only 7%of communication is based on the actual words we say. 38% comes from the tone of voice and 55% comes from body language. Being aware of your body language and of others around you will give a powerful edge to achieving your goals....in this case a bridezilla virus free wedding.

You may feel that you have not been infected with the bridezilla virus while planning your wedding or even on the wedding day. Your body, eyes, movements will either confirm or deny this feeling. Subconsciously the bridezilla virus will surface from our body language due to the stress of wedding planning. To keep the virus under control, being conscious of the following actions will certainly help.

- **Crossed arms and legs signal resistance to your ideas.** These unintentional physical barriers that signal you are not open to the other person's ideas, comments, or movements. Psychologically crossed legs and arms signals that a person is mentally, emotionally, and physically blocked off from what is in front of them.
- **Real smiles crinkle the eyes.** Your mouth may lie with a smile but your eyes will reveal your true feelings. Crinkling of the skin around the eyes is evident of a genuine like/love.
- **Copying others body language-** Mirroring others body language shows a bond with another person. It is a sign that a conversation is going well and that others are receptive to you.
- **Posture-** Standing straight and tall commands respect and promotes engagement. Slouching implies a timid, less powerful presence.
- **Eyes that lie-** On average, most people hold eye contact for seven to ten seconds, longer when they are listening or when talking. People whose stare is creepy, unblinking with a still body is a possible sign that they may be lying to you or they are zombies.
- **Raised eyebrows-** The three main emotions that raise your eyebrows are surprise, worry and fear. It is very difficult to raise your eyebrows in a relaxed casual conversation. If your eyebrows are raised in a situation that would not be one of the three main emotions, something is up.
- **Exaggerated nodding signals anxiety about approval-** When you are talking to someone and they are worried about what you think of them or their ability exaggerated nodding occurs.
- **A clenched jaw signals stress-** Stress is shown by a clenched jaw, tightened neck, or furrowed brow. These are all signs of discomfort.

Our body is a fascinating structure that is capable of many things. You may not be able to hide your feelings so it is best to be honest with yourself and others.

Takeover/Timing Tyrants

Your wedding day has arrived and instantly you are on a schedule. From your morning routine to beauty appointments and getting to the church on time is the goal for all brides. Friends and family will remind you of your timeline and schedule constantly during the wedding day. Just because you are the bride doesn't mean you can make people wait for you.

So how do you stick to a schedule? Simple, do not over book your time. Being late for even one event/appointment will snowball and cause the remaining events/appointments to be delayed. It only takes one delay to fuel the bridezilla virus to flare up. Expect everything to take longer than planned on the wedding day. Allow extra time for traffic while traveling. Be prepared that something will go wrong or not as planned. With proper organization, proper communication, and acceptance of what "is" and not what it should be, your day will be imperfect as expected (Yes, imperfect...nothing is ever perfect except on TV, internet, or Twitter.)

Getting yourself and key people in place for your event should be a job for the wedding coordinator. With your finely tuned plans laid out and key figures in place to execute your instructions down to the last word it happens...the takeover

tyrant lurks in the shadows waiting for an opportunity to take over your wedding.

Takeover tyrants appear in various forms. They could be your future in-laws, a picky bridesmaid, a know-it-all wedding guest, or even an overeager wedding guest with the best intentions. Take over tyrants feel that they are helping the bride by shielding the bride from any problems or issues that may arise.

As the bride, it is difficult to monitor every detail and be present for your wedding day. Therefore, you delegated this job to your wedding coordinator. When a takeover tyrant assumes a non-appointed position in your wedding it is best for the day of wedding coordinator to intercede on your behalf. The bridezilla virus could surface if you misread the intentions of the takeover tyrant. While you are most appreciative for their help and advice it is best to explain that you wanted them to enjoy and celebrate with you rather than work. If they insist on helping you on your most special

occasion, my advice is to refer them to the coordinator and have some small task for them to complete such as greeting guests like at a well-known superstore. Another task may be assisting those guests with special needs or aiding with breakdown or distribution/dismantling of wedding decorations.

The opportunities are endless for tasks that could be assigned. As I see it, it is a win -win situation. The takeover tyrant feels important, needed, and the bride has additional assistance for tasks that are not on the top of the list.

Lights, Camera, Action!

Your wedding day is here! Like a robot you awake, eat, shower, and run off to the hair stylist for that fabulous hair style and make-up application to give you that bridal glow. So far, the events of the day have not fully sunk in yet. The photographer has been clicking away candid photos of the pre-wedding preparation. The mood is very relaxed until you put on your wedding dress. Suddenly you realize that you have become the center of attention. If you are not one for being in the spotlight this may feel uncomfortable and frightening. The bridezilla virus can show its ugly symptoms due to fear and anxiety. There are several things that you can do to cope with your new-found fame.

The most nerve-wracking part of the wedding ceremony is the initial walk down the aisle. Truly all eyes are on your every move. The walk down the aisle can be frightening. To avoid anxiety, it is best to withdraw into a bubble. I am not suggesting withdrawing completely from the situation but focus your eyes on the prize...your fiancé waiting for you. A stress relieving tactic is to lean on those who will accompany you down the aisle for support.

Another nervous reaction to the hundreds of eyes watching you is to hide behind your bridal bouquet. Flowers
are meant to be an accessory to your wedding gown and not cover your face or your gown. This may seem insignificant at the time, but when your photos arrive you will see or will not see your gown and or face. The virus symptoms will flare up when your photographs do not reflect your memories. A few simple steps can be taken to avoid this but it takes practice.

There are several key factors to consider so you do not have that grab and go look:

- When presented your bouquet for the first time, stop and smell the flowers. Take in their beauty. Look at every part of the bouquet and decide if there is a side more photogenic than the other.

- Pick up your bouquet and feel its weight. The larger the bouquet the heavier it is. If the bouquet is a natural hand tied style, grasp the bouquet at the base of the flowers where the binding point will be. This will balance out the weight to make the bouquet more comfortable to carry. If your bouquet is constructed in a plastic holder, a handle will be provided. Once again grasp the bouquet at the top of the handle to distribute the weight.

- Hold your bouquet with relaxed hands and fingers. Do not tense your hands up with the grip of death on the bouquet, you will be in pain.

- Some state that when you hold your bouquet your thumbs should be at your belly button. This is too much to remember when the excitement of the moment overcomes you. I suggest you hold your bouquet with your arms fully extended downward in front of you. This may feel uncomfortable but when you begin to walk down the aisle your arms will rise to a comfortable level out of sheer fear. If you begin with your bouquet at your waist, your bouquet will rise as you walk and you will not see your face or dress.

- If you use the extended downward method of holding your bouquet your elbow will never bend to a 90-degree angle which is a no-no. Your elbow show be slightly bent emphasizing your waist.

- Look in the mirror. Be conscious of your arm position, keep your shoulders back, loosen up, and burn that memory in your head for the long walk down the aisle.

Keep the bridezilla virus dormant before, during, and especially after the ceremony. By taking a little time to practice with your bouquet before the ceremony it will save you years of regret.

You made it down the aisle without tripping, the ceremony has begun, and it is time for the vows. Committing yourself to your future spouse is a special time. Do not try to overdo it with an overwhelming production. Keep your vows to the point, sincere, and speak from the heart.

Another stressful time is the giving and presenting of the wedding rings. Swelling fingers is not uncommon to occur during the wedding ceremony. If the ring does not readily go on, do not force it! You may damage your hand and it could be uncomfortable and painful the rest of the day. Simply place the ring on the finger as far as it will go and be done. The ring will eventually fit just be patient.

Congratulations …. You did it! You are married and it is time to celebrate.

Stealing the Spotlight

It's your wedding day, everything is going as planned and then it happens…someone tries to steal your spotlight and turn your day into their own. It may be a bridesmaid trying to outshine the bride with something specific to wear, or a groomsman drinking too much prior to the ceremony and was unable to stand without swaying. It may be a guest being boisterous, obnoxious, or dancing without music being played. It could be a guest stuffing enough food or sweets into her purse/bag that you could live comfortably for more than a week. It may even be your mother or mother-in-law deciding to wear white/ivory to your wedding causing guests to wonder who the bride is. Any of the instances can push a bride over the edge to allow the bridezilla virus to emerge.

Your special day will be filled with guests celebrating your nuptials. Some may get carried away causing most to feel their actions are not appropriate for the situation. People are competitive in nature (especially women) and when someone starts to steal the spotlight it is best to take them aside and confront them right away. Be kind and not negative. If you focus on the negativity it will keep it alive and growing along with the bridezilla virus. Another approach to taking back your spotlight is to put a humorous spin on the event.

Take the edge off the incident and joke about it. Immediately turn the focus back to the main event…the wedding. It is difficult not to allow the bridezilla virus to surface. Your first instinct will be one of defense and anger. Step back, breathe, and remember if you let it bother you….it will. Don't ruin your event by unleashing the bridezilla virus.

You Ruined MY Wedding!

Your wedding day has arrived and suddenly the bridezilla virus appears. Something, someone, or even your significant other's actions may trigger you to be upset, angry, envious, or even irate.

When something does not go your way, we tend to be upset. When something goes wrong on your wedding day, the minor problem is intensified to epic proportions. Blaming others for mishaps that occur on your wedding day is easier than accepting that people are human and make mistakes, have poor judgment, and are insensitive at times.

There are several actions from others that would bug any person; but to a bride on the wedding day it is infuriating which fuels the bridezilla virus.

Some of the actions of others that may push you over the edge are:

- Hung over bridal party from the rehearsal dinner or bachelor party
- Showing up with a date who wasn't invited or liked
- Showing up late
- Incessantly texting or taking photos during the ceremony
- Speaking up during the ceremony
- Sticking a finger in the wedding cake
- Someone wearing white (or ivory) other than the bride
- Giving a "roast" rather than a toast
- Using your wedding to hook up at the event itself
- Drinking too much – it's a wedding celebration, not a fraternity party!
- Spilling anything on the bride
- Letting the kids run wild
- Telling the DJ to change the music
- Playing a joke on the bridal party
- Destroying property of the venue, wedding couple, or guests
- Having the police called to break up a fight
- Telling the bride, she could have looked better on her wedding day

Some of these issues would certainly cause anyone to be irate. The secret is not to allow the bridezilla virus to be in control of you. You and your fiancé planned a celebration you wanted to share with close friends and family. Take pride in known you have succeeded in accomplishing the main task of the day and that is marriage. The party is just a bonus! Do not let the actions of a select few people ruin your day. You worked hard to plan and execute it, now enjoy it. Worry about confronting anyone about any mishaps until after the wedding has ended.

Is it over yet?

Your wedding day is winding down and all the months or even years of planning produced an exceptional event. This is a bitter sweet ending to such a large part of your life. On one hand, you will have nothing to plan, control, or obsess over. On the other, you finally will have time for yourself and a sense of accomplishment. Wedding planning is an emotional rollercoaster that a couple rides not only for the duration of the wedding planning, but on the wedding day and through life.

Even with your best laid plans, there will be multiple questions for the couple on their wedding day. Some questions will be overwhelming, while others will be just annoying. An annoyed state of mind does not give you the right to be rude, insensitive, or mean. Do not let the bridezilla virus loose in the final hours. Just answer each question one at a time.

When the last song is played, the last drink poured, and the lights go on it's time to survey the damage and clean up. Your wedding is over and your life together as a married couple has begun.

The wedding experience is mentally and physically exhausting. The bridezilla virus may not end with the wedding celebration. The virus may linger several days to several weeks after the wedding.

The bridezilla virus is in all of us, only we can choose to let it surface. Always keep in mind that a wedding is not about the celebration; it is about the commitment between the two of you.

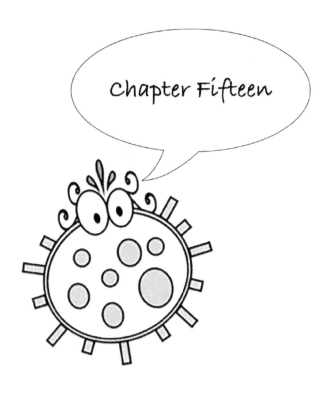

It's Never Really Over

Now What?

Your wedding experience is over and you are thrilled that you have survived your day without catching the bridezilla virus.... or so you think.

Your wedding celebration is never truly over. You will be reliving special moments of your wedding day repeatedly again for years to come. There are many tasks to complete after the actual wedding day. At this point, it is possible to have a relapse of the bridezilla virus if you delay the completion of each task. You are tired, even exhausted immediately following the celebration. All you want to do is relax. If you happen to go on a honeymoon immediately following your wedding celebration you will have some down time until you get home and back to reality. If not, take a few days to do nothing but recoup and recharge your body.

To ensure the bridezilla virus does not make an encore begin the following tasks as soon as possible after the wedding:

- Thank you notes
  - Good etiquette is to have thank you notes mailed within 90 days of the wedding.
- Cleaning your wedding dress
  - Fresh stains are easier to clean than ones that have been sitting for a while.
- Toss/dispose of any wedding items not worth saving
  - Keep your favorite mementoes and dispose of the rest.
- Insuring your wedding rings
  - A lost ring is heartbreaking. Make it less painful with a replacement policy.
- Request copies of your marriage license
  - Have several copies available for any name change forms, insurance, or where proof of marriage is necessary

By finishing these small tasks, you will feel as sense of accomplishment and you will be able to move on to the next chapter of your life together.

Take it slow…don't rush into your next big project…house, baby, etc. Always be prepared and remember to use the three "C's" in life, they will never let you down. Failing to do so may lead you to becoming a "B" and it will not mean bridezilla!

Printed in Great Britain
by Amazon

34322432R00081